The Spell of the Rockies

THE HOME OF THE WHIRLWIND (p. 78)

The Spell
of the Rockies

By
Enos A. Mills

With Illustrations from Photographs
by the Author

Introduction and Notes by
James H. Pickering

University of Nebraska Press
Lincoln and London

Introduction and notes copyright © 1989 by the University of
Nebraska Press

First Bison Book Printing: 1989
Most recent printing indicated by the last digit below:
10 9 8 7 6 5 4 3 2 1

Library of Congress Cataloging-in-Publication Data
Mills, Enos Abijah, 1870–1922.
    The spell of the Rockies / by Enos A. Mills: with illustrations
 from photographs by the author: introduction and notes by
 James H. Pickering.
        p. cm.
    Reprint. Originally published: Boston: Houghton Mifflin, 1911.
    Bibliography: p.
    Includes index.
    ISBN 0-8032-8163-3 (alk. paper)
 1. Natural history—Rocky Mountains. 2. Rocky Mountains—
    Description and travel. 3. Colorado—Description and travel.
    I. Title
  QH104.5.R6—55 1989
508.78—dc20   89-33076   CIP

This Bison Book reproduces the 1911 edition published by Houghton
Mifflin Company. To this edition an introduction, a chronology, and
notes for the entire volume have been added.

To
B. W.

Contents

Illustrations

Illustrations

Introduction
By James H. Pickering

At the time that he published *The Spell of the Rockies* in 1911, Enos Mills (1870–1922) of Estes Park, Colorado, enjoyed a substantial reputation "as one of the foremost American nature writers" and as a leading spokesman for wilderness preservation.[1] Forty-one years old, Enos Mills was at the very height of his career.[2] The previous decade had been a full and increasingly successful one, and the prospects for his latest and most ambitious project, the creation of a new national park in the Estes Park region, looked equally bright.

Though Enos Mills was destined to become one of the most famous mountain outdoorsmen and nature writers of his generation, his beginnings were anything but auspicious. Born and raised on the family farm near Pleasanton, Kansas, Mills was a sickly youth whose weak constitution interrupted his formal education and left him ill-equipped for the rigors of farm life. When his health had not improved by adolescence, the boy was encouraged by the family doctor and by his mother to seek a cure in the mountains of Colorado. Accordingly, in 1884, at the age of fourteen, Enos Mills made his way by way of Kansas City to Denver, and from there some fifty miles northwest to the mountain valley known as Estes Park.[3] Mills's immediate destination was the mountain home of his father's cousin, the Reverend Elkanah Lamb (1832–1915), who since 1875 had been homesteading in a small upland valley beneath the dramatic east face of Longs Peak. By the time that young Mills arrived, Lamb was augmenting his salary as an itinerant minister of the Church of the United Bretheren by putting up tourists at his Longs Peak House and guiding them to the summit for five dollars a trip.[4]

Though Lamb and his wife took him under their care, Enos

Enos Mills and family. Taken shortly before Enos left Kansas in 1884. Enos Mills is at the far left in row two. Courtesy of Mrs. Dorr Yeager.

Mills needed little direct supervision. Almost immediately he set about building his own homestead cabin on an unclaimed parcel of land directly east of Longs Peak House and began to learn the ways of the mountains. Well before he came to purchase Lamb's holding in 1902 and transformed Longs Peak House into the world-renowned Longs Peak Inn, Enos Mills had surpassed Father Lamb and his son Carlyle as the preeminent guide to the peak. Eventually, he reached its summit some three hundred times in every season of the year, on forty occasions while climbing alone. If ever a man came to know and master his environment, it was Enos Mills.

The mountain regimen dramatically improved Mills's health, and by the age of seventeen he was strong enough to seek employment as a tool boy in the copper mines of Butte, Montana. For the next fifteen years Mills followed a mining career, first at the Anaconda Mine in Butte, where he worked himself up to the position of engineer, and later in the mines at Victor and Cripple Creek, Colorado. At five dollars a day, the pay was good, and the work schedule sufficiently flexible to allow Mills to indulge his growing interest in the out-of-doors. Winters of hard work underground financed summers of exploration and travel. Before the age of twenty-five, Mills had visited California's Death Valley, seen firsthand the wonders of Yosemite and Yellowstone, and journeyed twice to the great frontier of Alaska, where during a second visit in 1894, deserted by guides, he traveled alone from north of Chilkoot Pass south to Juneau, a trip of more than two hundred miles. He also met John Muir, the celebrated naturalist and wilderness defender.

The chance encounter with Muir on the beach near San Francisco in December 1889 was clearly the turning point of Enos Mills's life. Outdoor interests, pursued largely for their own sake, became galvanized into a passionate commitment on behalf of wilderness preservation. "I owe everything to Muir," he later told a reporter for Michigan's *Dearborn Independent*. "If it hadn't been for him I would have been a mere gypsy. He told me to systematize my knowledge and that then I would be able to write. . . . He asked me questions about myself and my ambition and he advised me to study nature at every opportunity, everywhere, and to practice writing and speaking so I could tell what I saw."[5]

The decade that followed was one of immense personal growth. When he was not working in the mines, or experiencing nature directly, Mills was reading and writing. Books became his friends and constant companions. At first they were borrowed from the public library at Butte; later, as he could afford them, they were purchased. Eventually Mills amassed a good-sized collection which lined the walls of the three-room cabin behind Longs Peak Inn that served as his private study and workshop. There one could find literature by Shakespeare, Cervantes, Dickens, Thackeray, Byron, Stevenson, Scott, Emerson, Irving and Whitman; the nature writings of Thoreau, Burroughs, and Muir; books of travel and history; and philosophical and scientific works by such important nineteenth-century thinkers as Darwin, Huxley, Tyndall, Spencer, and Ingersoll.

Writing proficiency proved more difficult to achieve. Enos Mills quite literally taught himself to write, using the time-honored method of a journal or commonplace book into which he dutifully copied and stored away for future use items of information and bits of wisdom gleaned from his reading. These journals served as a convenient place to write out practice essays on a variety of topics. A number of these early literary efforts survive among the Enos Mills Papers. Painfully labored, they are noteworthy primarily because they remind us that as a writer, as in virtually everything he undertook, Enos Mills was a self-made man. Though he would never achieve great literary distinction, Mills would in time become a competent writer, able to tell an interesting and entertaining story in clear, vigorous language, and, more importantly, to sell for profit virtually everything he wrote.

Mills launched his career as a writer during the summer of 1896 by furnishing the *Denver Republican* with newsworthy items gathered from among the widely scattered hotels and ranches that formed the beginnings of Estes Park's resort industry. In the process Mills also collected the stories and reminiscences about Estes Park's early settlers that would go into his first published book, *The Story of Estes Park and a Guide Book* (1905).[6] Other publications followed, and by the time he bought out the Lambs and established Longs Peak Inn in 1902, Enos Mills had become a regular contributor to such well-known national big-circulation magazines as the *Saturday Evening Post, Atlantic, World's Work, Colliers, Harper's, Craftsman, Sunset, Country Life in America, Youth's Companion,* and *American Boy.* These magazines not only provided an outlet for Mills's wilderness message, with its emphasis on preservation and the need for national parks, but provided him with sufficient income to carry that message across the country.

As a naturalist, Enos Mills lacked formal scientific training. He was not particularly systematic in his approach. Rather, Mills's essential gift—one for which he was much admired—was that of a close and accurate observer. Possessed with a good eye and a keen imagination, Mills knew how to isolate the facts of nature and how to make those facts interesting by simply and directly relating them to the experience of his readers and listeners. For Mills, no less than for his eastern contemporary John Burroughs, "The facts of natural history become interesting the moment they become facts of human history. All the ways of the wild creatures in getting on in the world interest us, because we have our own ways of getting on in the world. All their essential economies, antagonisms, failures, devices, appeal to us for the same reason."[7]

Like Thoreau, Burroughs, and Muir, Mills had a strong and appreciative sense of man's interconnectedness with the natural world. This felt sense of kinship, in fact, sometimes led Mills astray. There is the tendency in his early writing, for example, to endow animals and birds with human psychology, and thereby commit the sin that Burroughs, Roosevelt, and others scornfully referred to as "nature faking." When he did so—when he falsified natural facts by humanizing them—Mills almost invariably slipped into sentimentality. But these were minor flaws. Enos Mills was an intensely curious man and, like the best nature writers, demonstrated that no experience was too small or too insignificant to catch his attention and reflection—from the homely facts of life in a beaver colony to the terrifying sublimity of a lightning storm on the heights. Enthusiasm for experience is felt everywhere in Mills's writing and it was this enthusiasm, remembered and recorded in the tranquility of the bachelor's study behind Longs Peak Inn, that strongly appealed to the middle-class audience for which he wrote.

Enos Mills's reputation might well have remained a regional

one had it not been for two closely related events that greatly expanded his audience and shaped its response. The first of these events occurred in late 1902, when Mills accepted the invitation of Louis G. Carpenter, the pioneering irrigation engineer then heading the State Irrigation Department, to serve as Colorado's official State Snow Observer. In this capacity, which lasted for some four seasons, 1903 to 1906, it became Mills's task to snowshoe the upper slopes of the Rockies, measuring the snow accumulation in order to anticipate the spring and summer runoffs that were so critical to farmers along the Front Range. It was a colorful and highly romantic sort of life, and one that Mills quickly learned to exploit to the advantage of his own reputation and career. "Snow observers," Mills told a reporter for the *Denver Times* in January 1904, "must go beyond the trails, climb the heights and traverse the wilds through all kinds of weather. They experience an amusing variety of conveyances, eat strange food and lodge in the best and in the worst of quarters. The work has roughness and its dangers, but there is abundance of life and fun in it."[8] "On these trips," Mills recalled, "I wore medium weight woolen underwear, overalls, and a canvas coat. While on snowshoes I have my feet in German socks and arctic overshoes. I carry a camera, a barometer, thermometer, compass and a folding axe. The only food I carry is either raisins or peanuts. I eat lightly while on the go, and can if necessary live for a week upon a pound of raisins. I have many times travelled for three days in succession without eating a bite."[9] The free and easy approach to wilderness life celebrated here became the essential ingredient of the persona that Mills would present to the nation. Forever afterwards he would be Enos Mills of Colorado, "a plain, simple man of the mountains . . . the woodland sage of Estes Park,"[10] the embodiment of a new kind of western outdoor hero: a man who in the service of wilderness ecology and preservation reported with simplicity, directness, and truth his exciting, often awe-inspiring and perilous, encounters with nature.

The second critical event of the decade followed closely upon the first. The publicity he received as Colorado's winter "Snow Man" and as a writer-naturalist brought Mills to the attention of President Theodore Roosevelt and Gifford Pinchot, the ambitious head of Roosevelt's new Forest Service. Forest conservation ranked high on the Roosevelt agenda, but like all new agendas—particularly one that challenged entrenched timber, farming, and mining interests—it needed broad public support in order to succeed. In Enos Mills, Roosevelt identified a nearly ideal advocate. In January 1907, Mills assumed the post of special "Government Lecturer on Forestry" with an assignment to spread the gospel of forest conservation and the recreational and aesthetic uses of America's endangered wilderness areas. Mills served in this capacity from January 1907 to May 1909 at a salary of $2,400 a year plus expenses. Pinchot and his Forest Service got their money's worth. Medium-sized and athletic, with a ruddy face and a very broad forehead, surmounted by a veritable shock of carrot-colored hair, Mills took to the lecture platform with a gusto and success that must have surprised even himself. He appeared before high school and college groups, teacher's organizations, women's clubs, civic and business meetings, before anyone, in short, willing to tender an invitation.

The pace he set was a frenetic one. During the period October 6 to December 29, 1908, for example, Mills gave some fifty-four lectures in fourteen different states. His subject was almost exclusively the use and misuse of trees, and everywhere he went the response was gratifyingly favorable. The comments of a writer for the *Omaha World Herald* are typical:

> Endowed with a rare gift of direct expression and with a reverence for nature not surpassed by John Burroughs himself, Mr. Mills revealed the utilitarian blessing of trees not more fully and convincingly than he did their esthetic value. He is one of those men in whom the scientist is blended with the artist, a person who sees with the heart as well as with an accurate eye. Moreover, his talk is flavored with a subtle western humor which enhances the effective mission which he has been commissioned to fulfill, in spreading the doctrine of tree planting and the preservation of forests.[11]

"Mr. Mills' talk was not only instructive, but intensely interesting," the *North Georgia Citizen* reported in its edition of January 23, 1908. "Without any attempt at oratory (or prepared notes of any

Longs Peak Inn. At the right is the original cabin that served as Elkanah Lamb's Longs Peak House. Courtesy of the State Historical Society of Colorado.

kind), he held a large audience with his rapid flow of words, interspersing quaint and humorous sayings with facts in reference to the forests."[12]

When Enos Mills was not pursuing his crusade to save the nation's forests, he was back home in Longs Peak Valley, that special place which served as inspiration and renewal. Here at Longs Peak Inn, in the heart of the natural world he knew best, Mills presided as genial summer host to hundreds of Americans who returned year after year to partake of his famous hospitality. The Inn itself never failed to impress the first-time visitor. "The main building is a wonder," enthused one guest in 1913.

It is all of logs and native woods in their original rustic shapes. There is a great big front room, office or lobby as it is called in town. Here is a huge fire-place of rustic stone, where a fire burns every night in the year. All about are rustic pieces of furniture made of curious old stumps, and knots and crooked sticks and strange timber growths. . . .

There is a great hospitable porch, a unique stair-case, a curious little post office, and a big cheerful dining room. Around about are the dozen or more log cabins of similar style. Some of these "cabins" have as many as ten rooms and one even has city style baths and steam heat—probably reserved for Boston people. Think of a steam heated log cabin in the mountain wilderness!

With all this goes a dining room service equal to any first-class city hotel—far better than that—equal in fact to the old farm house fare for on the place is produced the milk and cream and butter and chickens and eggs and vegetables that satisfy so well your Estes Park appetite.

This I did not see, but I was told that in the evening in the large front room the guests gather about the big old fire-place for an after dinner talk. Mr. Mills often comes in and talks on Mountain experience and adventure and of the many things one learns out in the wilds. And knowing how well he writes of all these things one can easily imagine how interesting one would find an evening with Mr. Mills before that fine, thick, old fire-place.

Off to one side of the group, over against a little forest, is the cabin which Mr. Mills calls his workshop. Here he works, and

Enos Mills and Scotch. Longs Peak Inn, c. 1909.
Courtesy of the State Historical Society of Colorado.

studies and writes. It is full of books, and unusual nature antiques, and rare photographs of mountain scenes and mountain animals.[13]

Operated exclusively as a "non-tip house," Longs Peak Inn perfectly mirrored the personality and convictions of its owner-proprietor. Mills's hand was everywhere apparent, from the "pithy and significant" signs that greeted arriving guests ("What Do You Want With an Armful of Wild Flowers?") to the thrice weekly nature talks delivered from the Inn's split-log stairs, the guided walks to nearby beaver ponds, and the strict house rules prohibiting "dancing, cards, and music in the Inn, because these were all lesser gods."[14] Mills's goal both as innkeeper and author was education and entertainment. At Longs Peak Inn there was plenty of both. There were hikes up Longs Peak, into nearby Wild Basin, or to dozens of other scenic places, horseback riding, fishing, tennis; evening bonfires and fireside talks, complete with toasted marshmallows, popcorn, and fudge; and sunny, cloudless days that began with morning sessions of beaver and bird watching and ended with moonlight walks to the top of Twin Sister Mountain across from the Inn to watch the sun rise over the eastern plains.

The year Mills left the employ of Forest Service proved to be a particularly important one. It saw the publication in March of Mills's first book of collected essays, *Wild Life on the Rockies*, an event made particularly significant by the fact that it was issued by Houghton Mifflin, the established Boston house that also published the works of John Muir and John Burroughs. The year 1909 also marked the beginnings of Mills's six-year battle for the establishment of Rocky Mountain National Park—an experience that he would call "the most strenuous and growth-compelling occupation I have ever followed" and "the achievement of my life." The role of promoter and lobbyist played by Mills throughout this long and protracted campaign proved to be a decisive one and the epithet he earned, "Father of Rocky Mountain National Park," was well deserved.[15]

The Spell of the Rockies, which Mills published in 1911 at $1.75, is in both format and content a sequel to *Wild Life on the Rockies*.[16] In its eighteen sketches and essays, a collection that the *Chicago Herald* pronounced "even better than its predecessor,"[17] Mills continued to do what he did best: tell good and convincing stories in a simple, straightforward way that made his book "a fit companion at an open fireplace on a winter's night."[18] "This is a book about the Rockies," remarked one reviewer—"not a guide book in any sense, but a book of observation and adventure and study and play. The mountains, the forests, the great forces that make scenery and soil, the animals, the birds, the avalanches, the landslides, the blizzards—these are the characters which move across the pages of this true story, which, although it is sober in truth, is a hundred times more interesting than most fiction."[19]

Not surprisingly, reviewers were very much impressed by Mills's stories of tight adventure in high places. "He has the gift of animated description," reported the *Milwaukee Free Press*; "his diction is tense, graphic and pictorial; the adventures he has to relate are wholly out of the ordinary. 'Racing an Avalanche,' 'Mountain Top Weather,' and 'Alone with a Landslide,' are three thrillers as stirring as ever came from a vivacious pen describing unprecedented and ultrahazardous predicaments."[20] Others noted the quieter, more contemplative Mills who could spend hours behind a boulder watching the activity in a beaver colony or take the whole of a calm, sunny morning watching a solitary bighorn sheep feeding among the rocks. Of all the favorable comments received, probably none pleased Mills himself more than the assurance by a writer for the *Chicago Inter-Ocean* that this book, together with *Wild Life on the Rockies*, gave Mills "a place in the first rank of American nature writers and showed him to be the chosen interpreter of the Rockies as surely as is John Muir the interpreter of the Sierras."[21]

As the modern reader will discover, *The Spell of the Rockies* wears surprisingly well, even after three-quarters of a century. Though some of Mills's sketches and essays may now seem a bit quaint or dated, the qualities that appealed most to Mills own contemporaries continue to appeal to us as well: his fresh and contagious enthusiasm for his subject, his adventurous, thoroughly engaged, yet playful approach to experience, and his deeply-held sense of the interconnectness and continuity of the natural world that points the way to still higher appreciation.

Enos Mills died a premature death on the evening of September 21, 1922. The immediate cause was blood poisoning occasioned by a severe abscess of the teeth. He was only fifty-two years old, a husband for a scant four years, a father for three. Following a simple service at the Inn, Mills was interred across the road closeby the homestead cabin he had erected in 1885–86. Tributes came in from across the nation, many of them eloquent in their praise of the man and his achievements. The remarks of Dean Babcock, an artist who had a home in Longs Peak Valley not far from the Inn, well summarized the view of those who had been privileged to enjoy Mills's company: "His friends and neighbors knew him to be a man of peculiar originality and force of character. Those who were fortunate enough to travel some of the long and difficult trails of the western mountains under his guidance might have observed his tireless energy, his resourcefulness, and his extraordinary woodcraft which combined with the primitive and unerring instinct of the Indian, the keen insight of the scientific observer."[22]

Notes

1. Unsigned review of *The Spell of the Rockies*, *New York Journal*, March 24, 1912, Enos Mills Papers, Western History Department, Denver Public Library. This repository of materials, consisting of an eclectic assortment of manuscripts, correspondence, speeches, biographical data, and clippings and articles by and about Enos Mills, was presented to the Denver Public Library by Mills's widow, Esther Burnell Mills (1889–1946). Hereafter cited as the Enos Mills Papers.

Though Mills's books were surprisingly widely reviewed, their sales, though respectable, were not spectacular. Surviving records at Houghton Mifflin reveal the following sales figures: *Wild Life on the Rockies* (1909), 21,941 copies; *The Spell of the Rockies* (1911), 12,597; *In Beaver World* (1913), 7,381; *The Story of a Thousand-Year Pine* (1914), 81,720; *The Story of Scotch* (1916), 11,555; *Your National Parks* (1917), 6,428; and *The Grizzly: Our Greatest Wild Animal* (1919), 7,298.

Nevertheless, Houghton Mifflin sales records also demonstrate that

Mills more than held his own when compared to John Burroughs and John Muir, the two contemporary writers with whom he is most often classed. Only three of Muir's titles—*Stickeen* (1909), *My First Summer in the Sierra* (1911), and *The Story of My Boyhood and Youth* (1913)—sold more copies than Mills's *Wild Life on the Rockies*. Only *Stickeen*, in fact, outsold Mills's *The Story of A Thousand-Year Pine*. Of Burroughs's many titles, only two—*Riverby* (1894) and *Bird and Bough* (1906)—sold more than 10,000 copies (they sold 12,788 and 10,341 copies, respectively). If these sales records are correct, they serve to validate the extent of Mills's own contemporary reputation.

That reputation did not, of course, rest upon the sale of books alone, but rather was the cumulative result of Mills's writings, including his hundreds of magazine and newspaper articles, and the result of his many lectures and personal appearances. A number of his writings went through a series of incarnations. For example, "The Story of Scotch" began as a chapter ("Faithful Scotch") in *Wild Life on the Rockies*, appeared again as magazine article published in the May 1, 1912, issue of *Country Life in America*, and was then published separately in book form by Houghton Mifflin in 1916.

2. For a fuller, more detailed account of Enos Mills's life and career see my introduction and notes to Mills's *Wild Life on the Rockies* (Lincoln: University of Nebraska Press, 1988), pp. xi–xlix. See also the chronology that follows this introduction.

3. Estes Park took its name from Joel Estes (1806–1875), a Missourian, who in mid-October of 1859, while on an exploring expedition with one of his sons, became the first known white man to enter the scenic valley that would soon bear his name. Estes liked the place, erected two cabins and a corral on what is now lower Fish Creek Road (at a spot near where it intersects Route 34, the road from Lyons), and proceeded to raise cattle. Joel and Patsy Estes also took in visitors, usually hunters who came to the valley in search of big game. William Byers, founding editor of the *Rocky Mountain News*, stayed with Estes and his family in August 1864, on the eve of his unsuccessful attempt to make the first recorded ascent of Longs Peak, and subsequently named the mountain valley after his hosts. Estes himself left the park in April 1866, never to return. The best account of Joel Estes and the early history of Estes Park is found in C. W. Bucholtz, *Rocky Mountain National Park: A History* (Boulder: Colorado Associated University Press, 1983).

4. "If they would not pay for spiritual guidance," the Reverend Lamb recalled in his memoirs, "I compelled them to divide for material elevation." Elkanah J. Lamb, *Memories of the Past and Thoughts of the Future* (United Brethren Publishing House, 1906), p. 166.

5. Fred L. Holmes, "Enos A. Mills—Nature Guide and Author," *Dearborn Independent*, c. 1921, Enos Mills Papers.

6. Mills had this slender volume of local history privately published by the Outdoor Life Publishing Company of Denver. Intended primarily for the Estes Park tourist trade and sold at the Inn, it went through three revisions during Mills's own lifetime and was subsequently revised by his wife and daughter. An edition was published by Doubleday, Page and Company in 1924.

7. John Burroughs, *Field and Study* (Boston: Houghton Mifflin Company, 1919), p. 193.

8. Quoted in unsigned Review, *Denver Times*, January 16, 1904, Enos Mills Papers.

9. Unsigned and undated news article, Enos Mills Papers.

10. Unsigned Review, *Colorado Springs Gazette*, December 12, 1913, Enos Mills Papers.

11. Unsigned review, *Omaha World Herald*, April 24, 1907, Enos Mills Papers.

12. Unsigned review, *North Georgia Citizen*, January 23, 1908, Enos Mills Papers.

13. G. U. H., "Long's Peak Inn and Mr. Enos A. Mills" (1913), Enos Mills Papers. Mills expanded Longs Peak Inn in 1916. At its height the Inn could serve upwards of a hundred guests and employed a staff of thirty-five, made up mostly of college students and schoolteachers. Following Mills's death in 1922, Longs Peak Inn was run for more than twenty years by his widow. She sold it in 1945, and a year later it burned to the ground.

14. Geneva Smithe, "Nature Guiding, A Project for Teachers," *The American Schoolmaster* (February 1923), Enos Mills Papers.

15. The bill establishing Rocky Mountain National Park was passed on January 18, 1915. The new park was formally dedicated at ceremonies in Horseshoe Park on September 4th of the same year, with Enos Mills serving as master of ceremonies. The story of Mills's role has already been told, most recently in my own introduction to *Wild Life on the Rockies*, cited above. Other major sources include Bucholtz, *Rocky Mountain National Park*, pp. 126–37; Lloyd K. Musselman, *Rocky Mountain National Park: Administrative History*, 1915–1965 (Washington: U.S. Department of the Interior, National Park Service, 1971), pp. 17–27; and, especially, Patricia M. Fazio, "Cragged Crusade: The Fight for Rocky Mountain National Park, 1909–1915," Master's thesis, University of Wyoming, Laramie, 1982. The fact that much of Mills's later career was consumed by an almost pathological battle with the National Park Service and those who administered the new Rocky Mountain National Park over the issue of an

exclusive transportation franchise that Mills viewed as unfair and monopolistic in no way diminishes his accomplishments. That Mills had a side to his personality that was contentious, rigidly uncompromising, and adversarial to the point of mean-spiritedness is clear enough from the surviving record. What is also clear is that Mills's quarrels and disputes (which included lawsuits) never influenced to any great extent the image and reputation held by the nation at large.

16. An English edition was subsequently published by the London firm of Constable and Company.

17. Unsigned review, *Chicago Herald*, December 12, 1911, Enos Mills Papers.

18. Review by James Barrett, *Denver Times*, December 7, 1911, Enos Mills Papers.

19. Unsigned review, *Charleston News and Courier*, October 27, 1912, Enos Mills Papers.

20. Unsigned review, *Milwaukee Free Press*, December 11, 1911, Enos Mills Papers.

21. Unsigned review, *Chicago Inter-Ocean*, November 25, 1911, Enos Mills Papers.

22. Dean Babcock, "Enos Mills—An Introduction," *The Pennant* (Canton, Illinois: March 1907), pp. 3–4, Enos Mills Papers. Babcock (1888–1969), a native of Illinois, first visited Estes Park in 1903 and returned again in the summers of 1904, 1905, and again in 1908, on each occasion making his headquarters at Longs Peak Inn. In 1910 Babcock built a permanent home, "The Ledges," to the north of the Inn.

Enos A. Mills: A Chronology

1870   April 22, Enos Abijah Mills born.

1884   Journeys to Estes Park, Colorado, by way of Kansas City and Denver. Works at Elkhorn Lodge.

1895   Works at Elkanah Lamb's Longs Peak House. First ascent of Longs Peak guided by Carlyle Lamb. Begins work on homestead cabin. Spends winter working on ranch in eastern Colorado.

1886   Works again for Lambs. Helps Carlyle Lamb construct Longs Peak Trail. Completes cabin.

1887   Summer in Estes Park. First solo ascent of Longs Peak. Travels to Butte, Montana, to work as tool boy at Anaconda copper mine.

1888   Summer in Estes Park. Promoted to miner at Butte.

1889   Guides first party to summit of Longs Peak. Fall, fire closes Anaconda mine. December, meets John Muir in San Francisco.

1890   Visits Death Valley, Yosemite, Sequoias, Virginia City and Reno; explores California coast south to San Diego. September, enrolls in Heald's Business College in San Francisco.

1891   January, returns to Butte to assume office position, but soon resigns. Spring, explores Yellowstone; remains for summer working with U.S. Geological Survey party.

1892   Spring, visits Alaska.

1893   Works in Ward, Colorado. Visits Chicago World's Fair and family in Kansas.

1894   Revisits Alaska. Deserted by guides, Mills walks alone more than two hundred miles from north of Chilkoot Pass south to Juneau.

1895   Fall, makes first forestry speech in Kansas City.

1896   February, addresses teachers' convention in Linn County, Kansas, on Peru, and receives twenty-five dollars. Begins reporting Estes Park resort news for Denver newspaper.

1896–   Spends winter working in mines at Victor and Cripple
1897   Creek.

1900   June 6, sails for Southampton to visit Paris Exposition with Elkanah Lamb. Visits Switzerland, Venice, Florence, Rome, and England. Sails for home on July 14.

1902   Purchases Longs Peak House from Carlyle Lamb. Scotch arrives as puppy.

1902–   December-January, as Snow Observer completes six-day,
1903   120-mile walk inspecting headwaters of the South Platte.

1903   February, makes first winter climb of Longs Peak, and journeys across Flattop Mountain to Grand Lake. June, repeats Elkanah Lamb's 1871 descent of East Face of Longs Peak. October, visits Mesa Verde.

1904   February, as Snow Observer completes seventy-mile trip inspecting headwaters of Grand, Big Thompson, and Michigan rivers.

1905   *The Story of Estes Park and a Guide Book* published. Fall-winter, undertakes lecture tour of east: including Kansas City, Memphis, New Orleans, Pittsburgh, Columbus, Chicago.

1906   June, main building of Longs Peak Inn burns while Enos is lecturing in St. Paul. Completes his last season as a Longs Peak guide. Makes thirty-two ascents during month of August. Lectures extensively. Meets John Burroughs.

1907   January, accepts Roosevelt's invitation to become special Government Lecturer on Forestry.

1908   Builds Timberline House on Longs Peak Trail, halfway to summit.

1909   May, resigns as Government Lecturer. *Wild Life on the Rockies* published. Fall, begins to campaign actively for a new national park in Estes Park area.

1910   June, Scotch is accidentally killed trying to extinguish the fuse on a charge of dynamite being used by a road crew near Longs Peak Inn.

1911   *The Spell of the Rockies* published.

1913   *In Beaver World* published.

1914   *The Story of a Thousand-Year Pine* published.

1915   January 16, Rocky Mountain National Park created by act of Congress. September 4, Park dedicated, with Enos Mills as master of ceremonies. *Rocky Mountain Wonderland* published.

1916   Enlarges Longs Peak Inn. *The Story of Scotch* published.

1917   January, attends National Parks Conference in Washington, presides at session discussing "The Recreational Use of National Parks." *Your National Parks* published.

1918   Marries Esther Burnell (1889–1946) on August 12 in ceremony at homestead cabin.

1919   Enda Mills born on April 27. Transportation concessions controversy begins. *Being Good to Bears: And Other True Animal Stories* and *The Grizzly: Our Greatest Wild Animal* published.

1920   *The Adventures of a Nature Guide* published.

1921   *Waiting in the Wilderness* published.

1922   January, injured in New York City subway collision. Enos

Mills dies on September 22. *Watched by Wild Animals* published.

1923   *Wild Animal Homesteads* published.

1924   *The Rocky Mountain National Park* published.

1926   *Romance of Geology* published.

1931   *Bird Memories of the Rockies* published.

Preface

ALTHOUGH I have been alone by a camp-fire in every State and Territory in the Union, with the exception of Rhode Island, the matter in this book is drawn almost entirely from my experiences in the Rocky Mountain region.

Some of the chapters have already appeared in magazines, and I am indebted to The Curtis Publishing Company, Doubleday, Page and Company, "Suburban Life," and "Recreation" for allowing me to reprint the papers which they have published. "Country Life in America" published "Racing an Avalanche," "Alone with a Landslide," and "A Rainy Day at the Stream's Source,"—the two last under the titles of "Alone with a Crumbling Mountain" and "At the Stream's Source." The "Saturday Evening Post" published "Little Conservationists," "Mountain-Top Weather," "The Forest Fire," "Insects in the Forest," "Doctor Woodpecker," and "The Fate of a

Preface

Tree Seed." "Suburban Life" published "Rob
of the Rockies" and "Little Boy Grizzly"; and
"Recreation" "Harvest Time with Beavers."

E. A. M.

Racing an Avalanche

Racing an Avalanche

I HAD gone into the San Juan Mountains during the first week in March to learn something of the laws which govern snow slides, to get a fuller idea of their power and destructiveness, and also with the hope of seeing them in wild, magnificent action. Everywhere, except on wind-swept points, the winter's snows lay deep. Conditions for slide movement were so favorable it seemed probable that, during the next few days at least, one would "run" or chute down every gulch that led from the summit. I climbed on skees well to the top of the range. By waiting on spurs and ridges I saw several thrilling exhibitions.

It was an exciting experience, but at the close of one great day the clear weather that had prevailed came to an end. From the table-like summit I watched hundreds of splendid clouds slowly advance, take their places, mass, and form fluffy seas in valley and cañons just

3

below my level. They submerged the low places in the plateau, and torn, silver-gray masses of mists surrounded crags and headlands. The sunset promised to be wonderful, but suddenly the mists came surging past my feet and threatened to shut out the view. Hurriedly climbing a promontory, I watched from it a many-colored sunset change and fade over mist-wreathed spires, and swelling, peak-torn seas. But the cloud-masses were rising, and suddenly points and peaks began to settle out of sight; then a dash of frosty mists, and my promontory sank into the sea. The light vanished from the heights, and I was caught in dense, frosty clouds and winter snows without a star.

I had left my skees at the foot of the promontory, and had climbed up by fingers and toes over the rocks without great difficulty. But on starting to return I could see only a few inches into the frosty, sheep's-wool clouds, and quickly found that trying to get down would be a perilous pastime. The side of the promontory stood over the steep walls of the plateau, and, not caring to be tumbled overboard by a slip, I concluded that sunrise from this point would probably be worth while.

It was not bitter cold, and I was comfortably dressed; however, it was necessary to do much dancing and arm-swinging to keep warm. Snow began to fall just after the clouds closed in, and it fell rapidly without a pause until near morning. Early in the evening I began a mental review of a number of subjects, mingling with these, from time to time, vigorous practice of gymnastics or calisthenics to help pass the night and to aid in keeping warm. The first subject I thought through was Arctic exploration; then I recalled all that my mind had retained of countless stories of mountain-climbing experiences; the contents of Tyndall's "Hours of Exercise in the Alps" was most clearly recalled. I was enjoying the poetry of Burns, when broken clouds and a glowing eastern sky claimed all attention until it was light enough to get off the promontory.

Planning to go down the west side, I crossed the table-like top, found, after many trials, a break in the enormous snow-cornice, and

started down the steep slope. It was a dangerous descent, for the rock was steep and smooth
as a wall, and was overladen with snow which
might slip at any moment. I descended slowly
and with great caution, so as not to start the
snow, as well as to guard against slipping and
losing control of myself. It was like descending
a mile of steep, snow-covered barn roof, —
nothing to lay hold of and omnipresent opportunity for slipping. A short distance below the
summit the clouds again were around me and I
could see only a short distance. I went sideways,
with my long skees, which I had now regained,
at right angles to the slope; slowly, a few inches
at a time, I eased myself down, planting one
skee firmly before I moved the other.

At last I reached a point where the wall was
sufficiently tilted to be called a slope, though it
was still too steep for safe coasting. The clouds
lifted and were floating away, while the sun
made the mountains of snow still whiter. I
paused to look back and up, to where the wall
ended in the blue sky, and could not understand how I had come safely down, even with

6

A SNOW-SLIDE REGION

Near Telluride, Colorado

Racing an Avalanche

the long tacks I had made, which showed clearly up to the snow-corniced, mist-shrouded crags at the summit. I had come down the side of a precipitous amphitheatre which rose a thousand feet or more above me. A short distance down the mountain, the slopes of this amphitheatre concentrated in a narrow gulch that extended two miles or more. Altogether it was like being in an enormous frying-pan lying face up. I was in the pan just above the place where the gulch handle joined.

It was a bad place to get out of, and thousands of tons of snow clinging to the steeps and sagging from corniced crests ready to slip, plunge down, and sweep the very spot on which I stood, showed most impressively that it was a perilous place to be in.

As I stood gazing upward and wondering how the snow ever could have held while I came down over it, there suddenly appeared on the upper steeps an upburst as from an explosion. Along several hundred feet of cornice, sprays and clouds of snow dashed and filled the air. An upward breeze curled and swept the top of this cloud over the crest in an inverted cascade.

All this showed for a few seconds until the snowy spray began to separate and vanish in the air. The snow-cloud settled downward and began to roll forward. Then monsters of massed snow appeared beneath the front of the cloud and plunged down the slopes. Wildly, grandly they dragged the entire snow-cloud in their wake. At the same instant the remainder of the snow-cornice was suddenly enveloped in another explosive snow-cloud effect.

A general slide had started. I whirled to escape, pointed my skees down the slope, — and went. In less than half a minute a tremendous snow avalanche, one hundred or perhaps two hundred feet deep and five or six hundred feet long, thundered over the spot where I had stood.

There was no chance to dodge, no time to climb out of the way. The only hope of escape lay in outrunning the magnificent monster. It came crashing and thundering after me as swift as a gale and more all-sweeping and destructive than an earthquake tidal wave.

Racing an Avalanche

I made a desperate start. Friction almost ceases to be a factor with skees on a snowy steep, and in less than a hundred yards I was going like the wind. For the first quarter of a mile, to the upper end of the gulch, was smooth coasting, and down this I shot, with the avalanche, comet-tailed with snow-dust, in close pursuit. A race for life was on.

The gulch down which I must go began with a rocky gorge and continued downward, an enormous U-shaped depression between high mountain-ridges. Here and there it expanded and then contracted, and it was broken with granite crags and ribs. It was piled and bristled with ten thousand fire-killed trees. To coast through all these snow-clad obstructions at breakneck speed would be taking the maximum number of life-and-death chances in the minimum amount of time. The worst of it all was that I had never been through the place. And bad enough, too, was the fact that a ridge thrust in from the left and completely hid the beginning of the gulch.

As I shot across the lower point of the ridge,

about to plunge blindly into the gorge, I thought of the possibility of becoming entangled in the hedge-like thickets of dwarfed, gnarled timberline trees. I also realized that I might dash against a cliff or plunge into a deep cañon. Of course I might strike an open way, but certain it was that I could not stop, nor see the beginning of the gorge, nor tell what I should strike when I shot over the ridge.

It was a second of most intense concern as I cleared the ridge blindly to go into what lay below and beyond. It was like leaping into the dark, and with the leap turning on the all-revealing light. As I cleared the ridge, there was just time to pull myself together for a forty-odd-foot leap across one arm of the horseshoe-shaped end of the gorge. In all my wild mountainside coasts on skees, never have I sped as swiftly as when I made this mad flight. As I shot through the air, I had a glimpse down into the pointed, snow-laden tops of a few tall fir trees that were firmly rooted among the rocks in the bottom of the gorge. Luckily I cleared the gorge and landed in a good place; but so narrowly did I miss the corner of a cliff that my shadow collided with it.

There was no time to bid farewell to fears when the slide started, nor to entertain them while running away from it. Instinct put me to flight; the situation set my wits working at their best, and, once started, I could neither stop nor look back; and so thick and fast did obstructions and dangers rise before me that only dimly and incidentally did I think of the oncoming danger behind.

I came down on the farther side of the gorge, to glance forward like an arrow. There was only an instant to shape my course and direct my flight across the second arm of the gorge, over which I leaped from a high place, sailing far above the snow-mantled trees and boulders in the bottom. My senses were keenly alert, and I remember noticing the shadows of the fir trees on the white snow and hearing while still in the air the brave, cheery notes of a chickadee; then the snowslide on my trail, less than an eighth of a mile behind, plunged into the gorge with a thundering crash. I came back to the snow on the lower side, and went skimming down the slope with the slide only a few seconds behind.

Fortunately most of the fallen masses of trees were buried, though a few broken limbs peeped through the snow to snag or trip me. How I ever dodged my way through the thickly standing tree growths is one feature of the experience that was too swift for recollection. Numerous factors presented themselves which should have done much to dispel mental procrastination and develop decision. There were scores of progressive propositions to decide within a few seconds; should I dodge that tree on the left side and duck under low limbs just beyond, or dodge to the right and scrape that pike of rocks? These, with my speed, required instant decision and action.

With almost uncontrollable rapidity I shot out into a small, nearly level glacier meadow, and had a brief rest from swift decisions and oncoming dangers. How relieved my weary brain felt, with nothing to decide about dodging! As though starved for thought material, I wondered if there were willows buried beneath

12

the snow. Sharp pains in my left hand compelled attention, and showed my left arm drawn
tightly against my breast, with fingers and
thumb spread to the fullest, and all their muscles tense.

The lower edge of the meadow was almost
blockaded with a dense growth of fire-killed
trees. Fortunately the easy slope here had so
checked my speed that I was able to dodge
safely through, but the heavy slide swept across
the meadow after me with undiminished speed,
and came crashing into the dead trees so close
to me that broken limbs were flung flying past
as I shot down off a steep moraine less than one
hundred feet ahead.

All the way down I had hoped to find a side
cañon into which I might dodge. I was going
too rapidly to enter the one I had seen. As I
coasted the moraine it flashed through my mind
that I had once heard a prospector say it was
only a quarter of a mile from Aspen Gulch up
to the meadows. Aspen Gulch came in on the
right, as the now slightly widening track seemed
to indicate.

The Spell of the Rockies

At the bottom of the moraine I was forced
between two trees that stood close together,
and a broken limb of one pierced my open coat
just beneath the left armhole, and slit the coat
to the bottom. My momentum and the resistance of the strong material gave me such a
shock that I was flung off my balance, and my
left skee smashed against a tree. Two feet of the
heel was broken off and the remainder split. I
managed to avoid falling, but had to check my
speed with my staff for fear of a worse accident.

Battling breakers with a broken oar or racing
with a broken skee are struggles of short dura-
tion. The slide did not slow down, and so closely
did it crowd me that, through the crashing of
trees as it struck them down, I could hear the
rocks and splintered timbers in its mass grinding together and thudding against obstructions
over which it swept. These sounds, and flying,
broken limbs cried to me "Faster!" and as I
started to descend another steep moraine, I
threw away my staff and "let go." I simply
flashed down the slope, dodged and rounded a

14

Racing an Avalanche

cliff, turned awkwardly into Aspen Gulch, and tumbled heels over head — into safety.

Then I picked myself up, to see the slide go by within twenty feet, with great broken trees sticking out of its side, and a snow-cloud dragging above.

Little Conservationists

Little Conservationists

*T*WENTY-FOUR years ago, while studying glaciation on the slope of Long's Peak, I
came upon a cluster of eight beaver houses.
These crude, conical mud huts were in a forest
pond far up on the mountainside. In this colony
of our first engineers were so many things of
interest that the fascinating study of the dead
Ice King's ruins and records was indefinitely
given up in order to observe Citizen Beaver's
works and ways.

The industrious beaver builds a permanent
home, keeps it clean and in repair, and beside
it stores food supplies for winter. He takes
thought for the morrow. These and other com-
mendable characteristics give him a place of
honor among the horde of homeless, hand-to-
mouth folk of the wild. His picturesque works
add a charm to nature and are helpful to man-
kind. His dams and ponds have saved vast

areas of soil, have checked many a flood, and helped to equalize stream-flow.

A pile of granite boulders on the edge of the pond stood several feet above the water-level, and from the top of these the entire colony and its operations could be seen. On these I spent days observing and enjoying the autumnal activities of Beaverdom.

It was the busiest time of the year for these industrious folk. General and extensive preparations were now being made for the long winter amid the mountain snows. A harvest of scores of trees was being gathered, and work on a new house was in progress, while the old houses were receiving repairs. It was a serene autumn day when I came into the picturesque village of these primitive people. The aspens were golden, the willows rusty, the grass tanned, and the pines were purring in the easy air.

The colony-site was in a small basin amid morainal débris at an altitude of nine thousand feet above the sea-level. I at once christened it the Moraine Colony. The scene was utterly wild. Peaks of crags and snow rose steeply and

MT. MEEKER

high above; all around crowded a dense ever-green forest of pine and spruce. A few small swamps reposed in this forest, while here and there in it bristled several gigantic windrows of boulders. A ragged belt of aspens surrounded the several ponds and separated the pines and spruces from the fringe of water-loving willows along the shores. There were three large ponds in succession and below these a number of smaller ones. The dams that formed the large ponds were willow-grown, earthy structures about four feet in height, and all sagged down stream. The houses were grouped in the middle pond, the largest one, the dam of which was more than three hundred feet long. Three of these lake dwellings stood near the upper mar-gin, close to where the brook poured in. The other five were clustered by the outlet, just be-low which a small willow-grown, boulder-dotted island lay between the divided waters of the stream.

A number of beavers were busy gnawing down aspens, while others cut the felled ones into sections, pushed and rolled the sections into the water, and then floated them to the harvest piles, one of which was being made beside each house. Some were quietly at work spreading a coat of mud on the outside of each house. This would freeze and defy the tooth and claw of the hungriest or the strongest predaceous enemy. Four beavers were leisurely lengthening and repairing a dam. A few worked singly, but most of them were in groups. All worked quietly and with apparent deliberation, but all were in motion, so that it was a busy scene. "To work like a beaver!" What a stirring exhibition of beaver industry and forethought I viewed from my boulder-pile!

At times upward of forty of them were in sight. Though there was a general coöperation, yet each one appeared to do his part without orders or direction. Time and again a group of workers completed a task and without pause silently moved off and began another. Everything appeared to go on mechanically. It produced a strange feeling to see so many workers doing so many kinds of work effectively and automatically. Again and again I listened for

Little Conservationists

the superintendent's voice; constantly I watched
to see the overseer move among them; but I
listened and watched in vain. Yet I feel that
some of the patriarchal fellows must have carried a general plan of the work, and that during
its progress orders and directions that I could
not comprehend were given from time to time.

The work was at its height a little before mid-
day. Nowadays it is rare for a beaver to work
in daylight. Men and guns have prevented daylight workers from leaving descendants. These
not only worked but played by day. One morning for more than an hour there was a general
frolic, in which the entire population appeared
to take part. They raced, dived, crowded in
general mix-ups, whacked the water with their
tails, wrestled, and dived again. There were
two or three play-centres, but the play went
on without intermission, and as their position
constantly changed, the merrymakers splashed
water all over the main pond before they calmed
down and in silence returned to work. I gave
most attention to the harvesters, who felled the
aspens and moved them, bodily or in sections,

by land and water to the harvest piles. One tree on the shore of the pond which was felled into the water was eight inches in diameter and fifteen feet high. Without having even a limb cut off, it was floated to the nearest harvest pile. Another, about the same size, which was procured some fifty feet from the water, was cut into four sections and its branches removed; then a single beaver would take a branch in his teeth, drag it to the water, and swim with it to a harvest pile. But four beavers united to transport the largest section to the water. They pushed with fore paws, with breasts, and with hips. Plainly it was too heavy for them. They paused. "Now they will go for help," I said to myself, "and I shall find out who the boss is." But to my astonishment one of them began to gnaw the piece in two, and two more began to clear a narrow way to the water, while the fourth set himself to cutting down another aspen. Good roads and open waterways are the rule, and perhaps the necessary rule, of beaver colonies.

I was impatient to have a close view of a

beaver cutting down a tree, and at last one came prospecting near where I was hidden. After a prolonged period of repose and possibly reflection he rose, gazed into the treetop, as though to see if it were entangled, then put his fore paws against the tree, spread his hind legs, sat back on his extended tail, and took a bite from the trunk. Everything in his actions suggested that his only intention was to devour the tree deliberately. He did most of the cutting from one side. Occasionally he pulled out a chip by leaning backward; sometimes he pried it out by tilting his head to the horizontal, forcing his lower front teeth behind it, then splitting it out by using his jaws as a lever. He was a trifle more than an hour in felling a four-inch tree; just before it fell he thudded the ground a few times with his tail and ran away.

I became deeply interested in this colony, which was situated within two miles of my cabin, and its nearness enabled me to be a frequent visitor and to follow closely its fortunes and misfortunes. About the hut-filled pond I lingered when it was covered with winter's white, when fringed with the gentian's blue, and while decked with the pond-lily's yellow glory.

Ruin befell it before my first visit ended. One morning, while watching from the boulder-pile, I noticed an occasional flake of ash dropping into the pond. Soon smoke scented the air, then came the awful and subdued roar of a forest fire. I fled, and from above the timber-line watched the storm-cloud of black smoke sweep furiously forward, bursting and closing to the terrible leaps of red and tattered flames. Before noon several thousand acres of forest were dead, all leaves and twigs were in ashes, all tree-trunks blistered and blackened.

The Moraine Colony was closely embowered in a pitchy forest. For a time the houses in the water must have been wrapped in flames of smelter heat. Could these mud houses stand this? The beavers themselves I knew would escape by sinking under the water. Next morning I went through the hot, smoky area and found every house cracked and crumbling; not one was inhabitable. Most serious of all was the total loss of the uncut food supply, when harvesting for winter had only begun.

Would these energetic people starve at home or would they try to find refuge in some other colony? Would they endeavor to find a grove that the fire had missed and there start anew? The intense heat had consumed almost every fibrous thing above the surface. The piles of garnered green aspen were charred to the water-line; all that remained of willow thickets and aspen groves were thousands of blackened pickets and points, acres of coarse charcoal stubble. It was a dreary, starving outlook for my furred friends.

I left the scene to explore the entire burned area. After wandering for hours amid ashes and charcoal, seeing here and there the seared carcass of a deer or some other wild animal, I came upon a beaver colony that had escaped the fire. It was in the midst of several acres of swampy ground that was covered with fire-resisting willows and aspens. The surrounding pine forest was not dense and the heat it produced in burning did no damage to the scattered beaver houses.

The Spell of the Rockies

From the top of a granite crag I surveyed the green scene of life and the surrounding sweep of desolation. Here and there a sodden log smouldered in the ashen distance and supported a tower of smoke in the still air. A few miles to the east, among the scattered trees of a rocky summit, the fire was burning itself out: to the west the sun was sinking behind crags and snow; near-by, on a blackened limb, a south-bound robin chattered volubly but hopelessly.

While I was listening, thinking, and watching, a mountain lion appeared and leaped lightly upon a block of granite. He was on my right, about one hundred feet away and about an equal distance from the shore of the nearest pond. He was interested in the approach of something. With a nervous switching of his tail he peered eagerly forward over the crown of the ridge just before him, and then crouched tensely and expectantly upon his rock.

A pine tree that had escaped the fire screened the place toward which the lion looked and where something evidently was approaching. While I was trying to discover what it could be, a coyote trotted into view. Without catching sight of the near-by lion, he suddenly stopped and fixed his gaze upon the point that so interested the crouching beast. The mystery was solved when thirty or forty beavers came hurrying into view. They had come from the ruined Moraine Colony.

I thought to myself that the coyote, stuffed as he must be with the seared flesh of fire-roasted victims, would not attack them; but a lion wants a fresh kill for every meal, and so I watched the movements of the latter. He adjusted his feet a trifle and made ready to spring. The beavers were getting close; but just as I was about to shout to frighten him the coyote leaped among them and began killing.

In the excitement of getting off the crag I narrowly escaped breaking my neck. Once on the ground I ran for the coyote, shouting wildly to frighten him off; but he was so intent upon killing that a violent kick in the ribs first made him aware of my presence. In anger and excitement he leaped at me with ugly teeth as he fled. The lion had disappeared, and by this time the beavers in the front ranks were jumping into the pond, while the others were awkwardly speeding down the slope. The coyote had killed three. If beavers have a language, surely that night the refugees related to their hospitable neighbors some thrilling experiences.

The next morning I returned to the Moraine Colony over the route followed by the refugees. Leaving their fire-ruined homes, they had followed the stream that issued from their ponds. In places the channel was so clogged with fire wreckage that they had followed alongside the water rather than in it, as is their wont. At one place they had hurriedly taken refuge in the stream. Coyote tracks in the scattered ashes explained this. But after going a short distance they had climbed from the water and again traveled the ashy earth.

Beavers, like fish, commonly follow water routes, but in times of emergency or in moments of audacity they will journey overland. To have followed this stream down to its first tributary, then up this to where the colony in which they found refuge was situated, would have required four miles of travel. Overland it was less than a mile. After following the stream for some distance, at just the right place they turned off, left the stream, and dared the overland dangers. How did they know the situation of the colony in the willows, or that it had escaped fire, and how could they have known the shortest, best way to it?

The morning after the arrival of the refugees, work was begun on two new houses and a dam, which was about sixty feet in length and built across a grassy open. Green cuttings of willow, aspen, and alder were used in its construction. Not a single stone or a handful of mud was used. When completed it appeared like a windrow of freshly raked shrubs. It was almost straight, but sagged a trifle downstream. Though the water filtered freely through, it flooded the flat above. As the two new houses could not shelter all the refugees, it is probable that some of them were sheltered in bank tunnels, while room for others may have been found in the old houses.

That winter the colony was raided by some

trappers; more than one hundred pelts were secured, and the colony was left in ruins and almost depopulated.

The Moraine Colony site was deserted for a long time. Eight years after the fire I returned to examine it. The willow growth about the ruins was almost as thrifty as when the fire came. A growth of aspen taller than one's head clung to the old shore-lines, while a close seedling growth of lodge-pole pine throve in the ashes of the old forest. One low mound, merry with blooming columbine, was the only house ruin to be seen.

The ponds were empty and every dam was broken. The stream, in rushing unobstructed through the ruins, had eroded deeply. This erosion revealed the records of ages, and showed that the old main dam had been built on the top of an older dam and a sediment-filled pond. The second dam was on top of an older one still. In the sediment of the oldest — the bottom pond — I found a spear-head, two charred logs, and the skull of a buffalo. Colonies of beaver, as well as those of men, are often found upon

Little Conservationists

sites that have a tragic history. Beavers, with
Omar, might say, —

> " When you and I behind the veil are past,
> Oh but the long long while the world shall last."

The next summer, 1893, the Moraine site was
resettled. During the first season the colonists
put in their time repairing dams and were content to live in holes. In autumn they gathered
no harvest, and no trace of them could be found
after the snow; so it is likely that they had
returned to winter in the colony whence they
had come. But early in the next spring there
were reinforced numbers of them at work establishing a permanent settlement. Three dams
were repaired, and in the autumn many of the
golden leaves that fell found lodgment in the
fresh plaster of two new houses.

Most beaver dams are built on the install-
ment plan, — are the result of growth. As the
pond fills with sediment, and the water becomes
shallower, the dam is built higher and, where
conditions require it, longer; or, as is often the
case, it may be raised and lengthened for the
purpose of raising or backing water to the trees

33

that are next to be harvested. The dams are made of sticks, small trees, sods, mud, stones, coal, grass, roots, — that is, combinations of these. The same may be said of the houses. For either house or dam the most convenient material is likely to be used. But this is not always the case; for the situation of the house, or what the dam may have to endure, evidently is sometimes considered, and apparently that kind of material is used that will best meet all the requirements.

Most beaver dams are so situated that they are destined earlier or later to accumulate sediment, trash, and fallen leaves, and become earthy; then they will, of course, be planted by Nature with grass, shrubby willows, and even trees. I have seen many trees with birds' nests in them standing on a beaver dam; yet the original dam had been composed almost entirely of sticks or stones.

Why do beavers want or need ponds? They have very heavy bodies and extremely short legs. On land they are slow and awkward and in the greatest danger from their enemies, —

Little Conservationists

wolves, lions, bears, and wildcats; but they are excellent swimmers, and in water they easily elude their enemies, and through it they conveniently bring their harvests home. Water is necessary for their existence, and to have this at all times compels the construction of dams and ponds.

In the new Moraine Colony one of the houses was torn to pieces by some animal, probably a bear. This was before Thanksgiving. About midwinter a prospector left his tunnel a few miles away, came to the colony, and dynamited a house, and "got seven of them." Next year two houses were built on the ruins of the two just fallen. That year's harvest-home was broken by deadly attacks of enemies. In gathering the harvest the beavers showed a preference for some aspens that were growing in a moist place about one hundred feet from the water. Whether it was the size of these or their peculiar flavor that determined their election in preference to nearer ones, I could not determine. One day, while several beavers were cutting here, they were surprised by a mountain lion, which leaped upon and killed one of the harvesters. The next day the lion surprised and killed another. Two or three days later a coyote killed one on the same blood-stained spot, and then overtook and killed two others as they fled for the water. I could not see these deadly attacks from the boulder-pile, but in each case the sight of flying beavers sent me rushing upon the scene, where I beheld the cause of their desperate retreat. But despite dangers they persisted until the last of these aspens was harvested. During the winter the bark was eaten from these, and the next season their clean wood was used in the walls of a new house.

One spring I several times visited a number of colonies while trying to determine the number of young brought forth at a birth. Six furry little fellows sunning themselves on top of their rude home were the first discovery; this was the twelfth of May. By the close of the month I had come in sight of many youngsters, and found the average number to be five. One mother proudly exhibited eight, while another, one who all winter had been harassed by trap-

Little Conservationists

pers and who lived in a burrow on the bank, could display but one. In the Moraine Colony the three sets of youngsters numbered two, three, and five. Great times these had as they were growing up. They played over the house, and such fun they had nosing and pushing each other off a large boulder into the water! A thousand merry ripples they sent to the shore as they raced, wrestled, and dived in the pond, both in the sunshine and in the shadows of the willows along the shore.

The beaver has a rich birthright, though born in a windowless hut of mud. Close to the primitive place of his birth the wild folk of both woods and water meet and often mingle; around it are the ever-changing, never-ending scenes and silences of the water or the shore. He grows up with the many-sided wild, playing amid the enameled flowers, the great boulders, — the Ice King's marbles, — and the fallen logs in the edge of the mysterious forest; learning to swim and slide; listening to the strong, harmonious stir of wind and water; living with the stars in the sky and the stars in the pond; beginning serious life when brilliant clouds of color enrich the hills; helping to harvest the trees that wear the robes of gold, while the birds go by for the southland in the reflective autumn days. If Mother Nature should ever call me to live upon another planet I could wish that I might be born a beaver, to inhabit a house in the water.

The autumn of the year when I watched the young beavers I had the pleasure of seeing some immigrants pass me *en route* for a new home in the Moraine Colony. Of course they may have been only visitors, or have come temporarily to assist in the harvesting; but I like to think of them as immigrants, and a number of things testified that immigrants they were. One evening I had long been lying on a boulder by the stream below the colony, waiting for a gift from the gods. It came. Out of the water within ten feet of me scrambled the most patriarchal, as well as the largest, beaver that I have ever seen. I wanted to take off my hat to him, I wanted to ask him to tell me the story of his life, but from long habit I simply lay still and watched and thought in silence. He was making a portage

A BEAVER HOUSE IN WINTER

round a cascade. As he scrambled up over the rocks, I noticed that he had but two fingers on his right hand. He was followed, in single file, by four others; one of these was minus a finger on the left hand. The next morning I read that five immigrants had arrived in the Moraine Colony. They had registered their footprints in the muddy margin of the lower pond. Had an agent been sent to invite these colonists, or had they come out of their own adventurous spirit? The day following their arrival I trailed them backward in the hope of learning whence they came and why they had moved. They had traveled in the water most of the time; but in places they had come out on the bank to go round a waterfall or to avoid an obstruction. Here and there I saw their tracks in the mud and traced them to a beaver settlement in which the houses and dams had been recently wrecked. A near-by rancher told me that he had been "making it hot" for all beavers in his meadow. During the next two years I occasionally saw this patriarchal beaver or his tracks thereabout.

It is the custom among old male beavers to

idle away two or three months of each summer
in exploring the neighboring brooks and streams.
But they never fail to return in time for autumn
activities. It thus becomes plain how, when an
old colony needs to move, some one in it knows
where to go and the route to follow.

I had enjoyed the ways of "our first engineers" for several years before it dawned upon
me that their works might be useful to man and
that the beaver might justly be called the first
conservationist. One dry winter the stream
through the Moraine Colony ran low and froze
to the bottom, and the only trout in it that
survived were those in the deep holes of these
beaver ponds. "Another demonstration of their
usefulness came one gray day. The easy rain of
two days ended in a heavy downpour and a
deluge of water on the mountainside above.
This mountain-slope was still barren from the
forest fire. It had but little to absorb or delay
the excess of water, which was speedily shed
into the stream below. Flooding down the
stream's channel came a roaring avalanche or
waterslide, with a rubbish-filled front that was

five or six feet high. This expanded as it rolled into the pond and swept far out on the sides, while the front, greatly lowered, rushed over the dam. Much of this water was caught and temporarily detained in the ponds, and by the time it poured over the last dam its volume was greatly reduced and its speed checked. The ponds had broken the rush and prevented a flood.

Every beaver pond is a settling-basin that takes sediment and soil from the water that passes through it. If this soil were carried down it would not only be lost, but it would clog the deep waterway, the river channel. Deposited in the pond, it will in time become productive. During past ages the millions of beaver dams in the United States have spread soil over thousands of square miles and rendered them productive. Beavers prepared the way for numerous forests and meadows, for countless orchards and peaceful, productive valleys.

The Moraine colonists gathered an unusually large harvest during the autumn of 1909. Seven hundred and thirty-two sapling aspens and several hundred willows were massed in the main pond by the largest house. This pile, which was mostly below the water-line, was three feet deep and one hundred and twenty-four feet in circumference. Would a new house be built this fall? This unusually large harvest plainly told that either children or immigrants had increased the population of the colony. Of course, a hard winter may also have been expected.

No; they were not to build a new house, but the old house by the harvest pile was to be enlarged. One day, just as the evening shadow of Long's Peak had covered the pond, I peeped over a log on top of the dam to watch the work. The house was only forty feet distant. Not a ripple stirred among the inverted peaks and pines in the clear, shadow-enameled pond. A lone beaver rose quietly in the scene from the water near the house. Swimming noiselessly, he made a circuit of the pond. Then for a time, and without any apparent purpose, he swam back and forth over a short, straight course; he moved leisurely, and occasionally made a shal-

Little Conservationists

low, quiet dive. He did not appear to be watching anything in particular or to have anything special on his mind. Yet his eyes may have been scouting for enemies and his mind may have been full of house plans. Finally he dived deeply, and the next I saw of him he was climbing up the side of the house addition with a pawful of mud.

By this time a number of beavers were swimming in the pond after the manner of the first one. Presently all began to work. The addition already stood more than two feet above the water-line. The top of this was crescent-shaped and was about seven feet long and half as wide. It was made mostly of mud, which was plentifully reinforced with willow cuttings and aspen sticks. For a time all the workers busied themselves in carrying mud and roots from the bottom of the pond and placing these on the slowly rising addition. Eleven were working at one time. By and by three swam ashore, each in a different direction and each a few seconds apart. After a minute or two they returned from the shore, each carrying or trailing a long willow.

These were dragged to the top of the addition, laid down, and trampled in the mud. Meantime the mud-carriers kept steadily at their work; again willows were brought, but this time four beavers went, and, as before, each was independent of the others. I did not see how this work could go on without some one bossing the thing, but I failed to detect any beaver acting as overseer. While there was general coöperation, each acted independently most of the time and sometimes was apparently oblivious of the others. These beavers simply worked, — slowly, silently, and steadily; and they were still working away methodically and with dignified deliberation when darkness hid them.

Most beaver houses are conical and round of outline. This house originally was slightly elliptical and measured forty-one feet in circumference. After enlargement it was almost a flattened ellipse and measured sixty-three feet in circumference. Generally I have found that small beaver houses are round and large ones elliptical.

One of the last large interesting works of the Moraine Colony was the making of a new pond.

Little Conservationists

This was made alongside the main pond and about fifty feet distant from it. A low ridge separated the two. As it was nearly one hundred feet from the stream, a ditch or canal was dug from the stream, below the main pond, to fill it. The new pond was made for the purpose of reaching with a waterway an aspen grove on its farther shore.

The making of the dam showed more forethought than the getting of the water into the pond. With the exception of aspen, no dam-making material such as beavers commonly use was to be found. The population of the colony was now large, while aspen, the chief food-supply, was becoming scarce. Would the beavers see far enough ahead to realize this? Evidently they did; at any rate not a single precious aspen was used in making the dam. Close to the dam-site was a supply of young lodge-pole pines; but it is against the tradition of the beaver to cut green pines or spruces. Two of these lodge-poles were cut, but evidently these pitchy, smelly things were not to the beavers' taste and no more of them were used.

The Spell of the Rockies

Not far away were scores of fire-killed trees, both standing and fallen. "Surely," I said to myself, when two dead chunks had been dragged into place, "they are not going to use this dead timber?" A beaver avoids gnawing dead wood; it is slow work, and besides is very hard on the teeth. Most of these dead trees were inconveniently large, and were fire-hardened and full of sand-filled weather-cracks; but contrary to all my years of observation, they, after long, hard labor, built an excellent dam from this material.

I have determined to do all I can to perpetuate the beaver, and I wish I could interest every man, woman, boy, and girl in the land to help in this. Beaver works are so picturesque and so useful to man that I trust this persistent practicer of conservation will not perish from the hills and mountains of our land. His growing scarcity is awakening some interest in him, and I hope and half believe that before many years every brook that is born on a great watershed will, as it goes swiftly, merrily singing down the

Little Conservationists

slopes toward the sea, pass through and be
steadied in a poetic pond that is made and will
be maintained by our patient, persistent, faithful
friend the beaver.

Harvest Time with Beavers

Harvest Time with Beavers

ONE autumn I watched a beaver colony and observed the customs of its primitive inhabitants as they gathered their harvest for winter. It was the Spruce Tree Colony, the most attractive one of the sixteen beaver municipalities on the big moraine on the slope of Long's Peak.

The first evening I concealed myself close to the beaver house by the edge of the pond. Just at sunset a large, aged beaver of striking, patriarchal appearance, rose in the water by the house and swam slowly, silently round the pond. He kept close to the shore and appeared to be scouting to see if an enemy lurked near. On completing the circuit of the pond, he climbed upon the end of a log that was thrust a few feet out into the water. Presently several other beaver appeared in the water close to the house. A few of these at once left the pond and nosed quietly about on the shore. The others swam about for some minutes and then joined their comrades on land, where all rested for a time.

Meanwhile the aged beaver had lifted a small aspen limb out of the water and was squatted on the log, leisurely eating bark. Before many minutes elapsed the other beaver became restless and finally started up the slope in a runway. They traveled slowly in single file and one by one vanished amid the tall sedge. The old beaver slipped noiselessly into the water, and a series of low waves pointed toward the house. It was dark as I stole away in silence for the night, and Mars was gently throbbing in the black water.

This was an old beaver settlement, and the numerous harvests gathered by its inhabitants had long since exhausted the near-by growths of aspen, the bark of which is the favorite food of North American beaver, though the bark of willow, cottonwood, alder, and birch is also eaten. An examination of the aspen supply, together with the lines of transportation, — the runways, canals, and ponds,—indicated that this year's harvest would have to be brought a long distance. The place it would come from was an aspen grove far up the slope, about a quarter of a mile distant from the main house, and perhaps a hundred and twenty feet above it. In this grove I cut three notches in the trunks of several trees to enable me to identify them whether in the garnered pile by a house or along the line of transportation to it.

The grounds of this colony occupied several acres on a terraced, moderately steep slope of a mountain moraine. Along one side rushed a swift stream on which the colonists maintained three but little used ponds. On the opposite side were the slope and summit of the moraine. There was a large pond at the bottom, and one or two small ponds, or water-filled basins, dotted each of the five terraces which rose above. The entire grounds were perforated with subterranean passageways or tunnels.

Beaver commonly fill their ponds by damming a brook or a river. But this colony obtained most of its water-supply from springs poured forth abundantly on the uppermost terrace, where the water was led into one pond and a number of basins. Overflowing from these, it either made a merry, tiny cascade or went to lubricate a slide on the short slopes which led to the ponds on the terrace below. The waters from all terraces were gathered into a large pond at the bottom. This pond measured six hundred feet in circumference. The crooked and almost encircling grass-grown dam was six feet high, and four hundred feet long. In its upper edge stood the main house, which was eighty feet high and forty feet in circumference. There was also another house on one of the terraces.

After notching the aspens I spent some time exploring the colony grounds and did not return to the marked trees until forty-eight hours had elapsed. Harvest had begun, and one of the largest notched trees had been felled and re-moved. Its gnawed stump was six inches in diameter and stood fifteen inches high. The limbs had been trimmed off, and a number of these lay scattered about the stump. The trunk, which must have been about eighteen feet long, had disappeared, cut into lengths of from three to six feet, probably, and started

54

toward the harvest pile. Wondering for which house these logs were intended, I followed, hoping to trace and trail them to the house, or find them *en route*. From the spot where they were cut, they had evidently been rolled down a steep, grassy seventy-foot slope, at the bottom of this dragged an equal distance over a level stretch among some lodge-pole pines, and then pushed or dragged along a narrow runway that had been cut through a rank growth of willows. Once through the willows, they were pushed into the uppermost pond. They were taken across this, forced over the dam on the opposite side, and shot down a slide into the pond which contained the smaller house. Only forty-eight hours before, the little logs which I was following were in a tree, and now I expected to find them by this house. It was good work to have got them here so quickly, I thought. But no logs could be found by the house or in the pond! The folks at this place had not yet laid up anything for winter. The logs must have gone farther.

On the opposite side of this pond I found where the logs had been dragged across the broad dam and then heaved into a long, wet slide which landed them in a small, shallow harbor in the grass. From this point a canal about eighty feet long ran around the brow of the terrace and ended at the top of a long slide which reached to the big pond. This canal was new and probably had been dug especially for this harvest. For sixty feet of its length it was quite regular in form and had an average width of thirty inches and a depth of fourteen. The mud dug in making it was piled evenly along the lower side. Altogether it looked more like the work of a careful man with a shovel than of beaver without tools. Seepage and overflow water from the ponds above filled and flowed slowly through it and out at the farther end, where it swept down the long slide into the big pond. Through this canal the logs had been taken one by one. At the farther end I found the butt-end log. It probably had been too heavy to heave out of the canal, but tracks in the mud indicated that there was a hard tussle before it was abandoned.

The pile of winter supplies was started. Close

A BEAVER CANAL

Length 334 feet, average depth 15 inches, average width 26 inches

to the big house a few aspen leaves fluttered on twigs in the water; evidently these twigs were attached to limbs or larger pieces of aspen that were piled beneath the surface. Could it be that the aspen which I had marked on the mountainside a quarter of a mile distant so short a time before, and which I had followed over slope and slide, canal and basin, was now piled on the bottom of this pond? I waded out into the water, prodded about with a pole, and found several smaller logs. Dragging one of these to the surface, I found there were three notches on it.

Evidently these heavy green tree cuttings had been sunk to the bottom simply by the piling of other similar cuttings upon them. With this heavy material in the still water a slight contact with the bottom would prevent the drifting of accumulating cuttings until a heavy pile could be formed. However, in deep or swift water I have noticed that an anchorage for the first few pieces was secured by placing these upon the lower slope of the house or against the dam.

The Spell of the Rockies

Scores of aspens were felled in the grove where the notched ones were. They were trimmed, cut into sections, and limbs, logs, and all taken over the route of the one I had followed, and at last placed in a pile beside the big house. This harvest gathering went on for a month. All about was busy, earnest preparation for winter. The squirrels from the tree-tops kept a rattling rain of cones on the leaf-strewn forest floor, the cheery chipmunk foraged and frolicked among the withered leaves and plants, while aspens with leaves of gold fell before the ivory sickles of the beaver. Splendid glimpses, grand views, I had of this strange harvest-home. How busy the beavers were! They were busy in the grove on the steep mountainside; they tugged logs along the runways; they hurried them across the water-basins, wrestled with them in canals, and merrily piled them by the rude house in the water. And I watched them through the changing hours; I saw their shadowy activity in the starry, silent night; I saw them hopefully leave home for the harvest groves in the serene twilight, and I watched

them working busily in the light of the noonday
sun.

Most of the aspens were cut off between
thirteen and fifteen inches above the ground.
A few stumps were less than five inches high,
while a number were four feet high. These high
cuttings were probably made from reclining
trunks of lodged aspens which were afterward
removed. The average diameter of the aspens
cut was four and one half inches at the top
of the stump. Numerous seedlings of an inch
diameter were cut, and the largest tree felled
for this harvest measured fourteen inches across
the stump. This had been laid low only a few
hours before I found it, and a bushel of white
chips and cuttings encircled the lifeless stump
like a wreath. In falling, the top had become
entangled in an alder thicket and lodged six
feet from the ground. It remained in this position for several days and was apparently abandoned; but the last time I went to see it the
alders which upheld it were being cut away.
Although the alders were thick upon the ground,
only those which had upheld the aspen had

been cut. It may be that the beaver which felled them looked and thought before they went ahead with the cutting.

Why had this and several other large aspens been left uncut in a place where all were convenient for harvest? All other neighboring aspens were cut years ago. One explanation is that the beaver realized that the tops of the aspens were entangled and interlocked in the limbs of crowding spruces and would not fall if cut off at the bottom. This and one other were the only large ones that were felled, and the tops of these had been recently released by the overturning of some spruces and the breaking of several branches on others. Other scattered large aspens were left uncut, but all of these were clasped in the arms of near-by spruces.

It was the habit of these colonists to transfer a tree to the harvest pile promptly after cutting it down. But one morning I found logs on slides and in canals, and unfinished work in the grove, as though everything had been suddenly dropped in the night when work was at its height. Coyotes had howled freely during the night, but this was not uncommon. In going over the grounds I found the explanation of this untidy work in a bear track and numerous wolf tracks, freshly moulded in the muddy places.

After the bulk of the harvest was gathered, I went one day to the opposite side of the moraine and briefly observed the methods of the Island beaver colony. The ways of the two colonies were in some things very different. In the Spruce Tree Colony the custom was to move the felled aspen promptly to the harvest pile. In the Island Colony the custom was to cut down most of the harvest before transporting any of it to the pile beside the house. Of the one hundred and sixty-two trees that had been felled for this harvest, one hundred and twenty-seven were still lying where they fell. However, the work of transporting was getting under way; a few logs were in the pile beside the house, and numerous others were scattered along the canals, runways, and slides between the house and the harvest grove.

There was more wasted labor, too, in the Island Colony. This was noticeable in the attempts that had been made to fell limb-en-tangled trees that could not fall. One five-inch aspen had three times been cut off at the bottom. The third cut was more than three feet from the ground, and was made by a beaver working from the top of a fallen log. Still this high-cut aspen refused to come down and there it hung like a collapsed balloon entangled in tree-tops.

Before the white man came it is probable that beaver did most of their work in the day-time. But at present, except in the most remote localities, day work is perilous. Prowling hunters have compelled most beaver to work at night. The Spruce Tree Colony was an isolated one, and occasionally its members worked and even played in the sunshine. Each day I secluded myself, kept still, and waited; and on a few occasions watched them as they worked in the light.

One windy day, just as I was unroping myself from the shaking limb of a spruce, four beaver were plodding along in single file beneath. They had come out of a hole between the roots of the spruce. At an aspen growth about fifty feet distant they separated. Though they had been closely assembled, each appeared utterly oblivious of the presence of the others. One squatted on the ground by an aspen, took a bite of bark out of it and ate leisurely. By and by he rose, clasped the aspen with fore paws and began to bite chips from it systematically. He was deliberately cutting it down. The most aged beaver waddled near an aspen, gazed into its top for a few seconds, then moved away about ten feet and started to fell a five-inch aspen. The one rejected was entangled at the top. Presently the third beaver selected a tree, and after some trouble to get comfortably seated, or squatted, also began cutting. The fourth beaver disappeared and I did not see him again. While I was looking for this one the huge, aged beaver whose venerable appearance had impressed me the first evening appeared on the scene. He came out of a hole beneath some spruces about a hundred feet distant. He looked neither to right nor to left, nor up nor down, as he ambled toward the aspen growth. When about halfway there he wheeled suddenly and took an uneasy survey of the open he had traversed, as though he had heard an enemy behind. Then with apparently stolid indifference he went on leisurely, and for a time paused among the cutters, which did nothing to indicate that they realized his presence. He ate some bark from a green limb on the ground, moved on, and went into the hole beneath me. He appeared so large that I afterward measured the distance between the two aspens where he paused. He was not less than three and a half feet long and probably weighed fifty pounds. He had all his toes; there was no white spot on his body; in fact, there was neither mark nor blemish by which I could positively identify him. Yet I feel that in my month around the colony I beheld the patriarch of the first evening in several scenes of action.

Sixty-seven minutes after the second beaver began cutting he made a brief pause; then he suddenly thudded the ground with his tail, hurriedly took out a few more chips, and ran away, with the other two beaver a little in

ASPENS CUT BY BEAVER

advance, just as his four-inch aspen settled over and then fell. All paused for a time close to the hole beneath me, and then the old beaver returned to his work. The one that had felled his tree followed closely and at once began on another aspen. The other beaver, with his aspen half cut off, went into the hole and did not again come out. By and by an old and a young beaver came out of the hole. The young one at once began cutting limbs off the recently felled aspen, while the other began work on the half-cut tree; but he ignored the work already done, and finally severed the trunk about four inches above the cut made by the other. Suddenly the old beaver whacked the ground and ran, but at thirty feet distant he paused and nervously thumped the ground with his tail, as his aspen slowly settled and fell. Then he went into the hole beneath me.

This year's harvest was so much larger than usual that it may be the population of this colony had been increased by the arrival of emigrants from a persecuted colony down in the valley. The total harvest numbered four hundred and forty-three trees. These made a harvest pile four feet high and ninety feet in circumference. A thick covering of willows was placed on top of the harvest pile, — I cannot tell for what reason unless it was to sink all the aspen below reach of the ice. This bulk of stores together with numerous roots of willow and water plants, which in the water are eaten from the bottom of the pond, would support a numerous beaver population through the days of ice and snow.

On the last tour through the colony everything was ready for the long and cold winter. Dams were in repair and ponds were brimming over with water, the fresh coats of mud on the houses were freezing to defy enemies, and a bountiful harvest was home. Harvest-gathering is full of hope and romance. What a joy it must be to every man or animal who has a hand in it! What a satisfaction, too, for all dependent upon a harvest, to know that there is abundance stored for all the frosty days!

The people of this wild, strange, picturesque colony had planned and prepared well. I wished

Harvest Time with Beavers

them a winter unvisited by cruel fate or foe, and trusted that when June came again the fat and furry young beaver would play with the aged one amid the tiger lilies in the shadows of the big spruce trees.

Mountain-Top Weather

Mountain-Top Weather

THE narrow Alpine zone of peaks and snow that forms the crest of the Rocky Mountains has its own individual elemental moods, its characteristic winds, its electrical and other peculiarities, and a climate of its own. Commonly its days are serene and sunny, but from time to time it has hail and snow and showers of wind-blown rain, cold as ice-water. It is subject to violent changes from clear, calm air to blizzard.

I have enjoyed these strange, silent heights in every season of the year. In climbing scores of these peaks, in crossing the passes, often on snowshoes, and in camping here and there on the skyline, I have encountered these climatic changes and had numerous strange experiences. From these experiences I realize that the transcontinental aviator, with this realm of peak and sky, will have some delightful as well as serious surprises. He will encounter stern conditions.

He may, like a storm-defying bird, be carried from his course by treacherous currents and battle with breakers or struggle in vain in the monstrous, invisible maelstroms that beset this ocean of air. Of these skyline factors the more imposing are wind, cold, clouds, rain, snow, and subtle, capricious electricity.

High winds are common across the summits of these mountains; and they are most prevalent in winter. Those of summer, though less frequent and much more short-lived, are a menace on account of their fury and the suddenness with which they surprise and sweep the heights.

Early one summer, while exploring a wide alpine moorland above the timber-line, I — and some others — had an experience with one of those sudden stormbursts. The region was utterly wild, but up to it straggling tourists occasionally rode for a view of the surrounding mountain world. All alone, I was studying the ways of the wild inhabitants of the heights. I had spent the calm, sunny morning in watching a solitary bighorn that was feeding among some boulders. He was aged, and he ate as though his teeth were poor and walked as though afflicted with rheumatism. Suddenly this patriarch forgot his age and fled precipitately, with almost the speed of frightened youth. I leaped upon a boulder to watch him, but was instantly knocked headlong by a wild blast of wind. In falling I caught sight of a straw hat and a wrecked umbrella falling out of the sky. Rising amid the pelting gale of flung hail, ice-water, and snow, I pushed my way in the teeth of the storm, hoping for shelter in the lee of a rock-pile about a hundred yards distant. A lady's disheveled hat blew by me, and with the howl of the wind came, almost drowned, excited human utterances. Nearing the rock-pile, I caught a vague view of a merry-go-round of man and horse, then a glimpse of the last gyration, in which an elderly Eastern gentleman parted company with a stampeded bronco.

Five tourists had ridden up in the sunshine to enjoy the heights, and the suddenness and fierceness of the storm had thrown them into a panic and stampeded their horses. They were drenched and severely chilled, and they were frightened. I made haste to tell them that the storm would be brief. While I was still trying to reassure them, the clouds commenced to dissolve and the sun came out. Presently all were watching the majestic soaring of two eagles up in the blue, while I went off to collect five scattered saddle-ponies that were contentedly feeding far away on the moor.

Though the winter winds are of slower development, they are more prolonged and are tempestuously powerful. Occasionally these winds blow for days; and where they follow a fall of snow they blow and whirl this about so wildly that the air is befogged for several hundred feet above the earth. So violently and thickly is the powdered snow flung about that a few minutes at a time is the longest that one can see or breathe in it. These high winter winds come out of the west in a deep, broad stratum that is far above most of the surface over which they blow. Commonly a high wind strikes the western slope of the Continental Divide a little below the altitude of eleven thousand feet. This striking throws it into fierce confusion. It rolls whirling up the steeps and frequently shoots far above the highest peaks. Across the passes it sweeps, roars down the cañons on the eastern slope, and rushes out across the plains. Though the western slope below eleven thousand feet is a calm zone, the entire eastern slope is being whipped and scourged by a flood of wind. Occasionally the temperature of these winds is warm.

These swift, insistent winds, torn, intercepted, and deflected by dashing against the broken skyline, produce currents, counter-currents, sleepy eddies, violent vertical whirls, and milling maelstroms that are tilted at every angle. In places there is a gale blowing upward, and here and there the air pours heavily down in an invisible but almost crushing air-fall.

One winter I placed an air-meter in Granite Pass, at twelve thousand feet altitude on the slope of Long's Peak. During the first high wind I fought my way up to read what the meter said. Both the meter and myself found the wind exceeded the speed limit. Emerging above the trees at timber-line, I had to face the unbroken fury of the gale as it swept down the slope from the heights above. The region was barren of snow. The wind dashed me with sandblasts and pelted me with gravel volleys that were almost unbearable. My face and wrists were bruised, and blood was drawn in many places where the gravel struck.

Seeking rest and shelter from this persistent punishment, I approached a crag and when only a few yards away was struck and overturned by the milling air-current around it. The air was so agitated around this crag that its churnings followed me, like disturbed water, under and behind the large rock-fragments, where shelter was hoped for but only partly secured.

On the last slope below the meter the wind simply played with me. I was overthrown, tripped, knocked down, blown explosively off my feet and dropped. Sometimes the wind dropped me heavily, but just as often it eased me down. I made no attempt to stand erect; most of the time this was impossible and at all times it was very dangerous. Now and then the wind rolled me as I lay resting upon a smooth

76

WIND-BLOWN TREES AT TIMBER-LINE

place. Advancing was akin to swimming a whirlpool or to wrestling one's way up a slope despite the ceaseless opposition of a vigorous, tireless opponent.

At last I crawled and climbed up to the buzzing cups of the meter. So swiftly were they rotating they formed a blurred circle, like a fast-revolving life-preserver. The meter showed that the wind was passing with a speed of from one hundred and sixty-five to one hundred and seventy miles an hour. The meter blew up — or, rather, flew to pieces — during a swifter spurt.

The wind so loudly ripped and roared round the top of the peak that I determined to scale the summit and experience its wildest and most eloquent efforts. All my strength and climbing knowledge were required to prevent my being literally blown out of converging rock channels through which the wind gushed; again and again I clung with all my might to avoid being torn from the ledges. Fortunately not a bruise was received, though many times this was narrowly avoided.

The Spell of the Rockies

The top of the peak, an area of between three and four acres and comparatively level, was in an easy eddy, almost a calm when compared with the wind's activities below and near by. Apparently the wind-current collided so forcefully with the western wall of the peak that it was thrown far above the summit before recovering to continue its way eastward; but against the resisting spurs and pinnacles a little below summit-level the wind roared, boomed, and crashed in its determined, passionate onsweep.

The better to hear this grand uproar, I advanced to the western edge of the summit. Here my hat was torn off, but not quite grasped, by the upshooting blast. It fell into the swirl above the summit and in large circles floated upward at slow speed, rising directly above the top of the peak. It rose and circled so slowly that I threw several stones at it, trying to knock it down before it rose out of range. The diameter of the circle through which it floated was about one hundred and fifty feet; when it had risen five, or perhaps six, hundred feet above the summit it suddenly tumbled over and over as though about to fall, but instead of falling it sailed off toward the east as though a carrier pigeon hurrying for a known and definite place in the horizon.

Some of the gulf-streams, hell-gates, whirl-pools, rough channels, and dangerous tides in the sea of air either are in fixed places or adjust themselves to winds from a different quarter so definitely that their location can be told by considering them in connection with the direction of the wind. Thus the sea of air may be partly charted and the position of some of its dangerous places, even in mountain-top oceans, positively known.

However, there are dangerous mountain-top winds of one kind, or, more properly, numerous local air-blasts, that are sometimes created within these high winds, that do not appear to have any habits. It would be easier to tell where the next thunderbolt would fall than where the next one of these would explode. One of these might be called a cannon wind. An old prospector, who had experienced countless high winds among the crags, once stated that high, gusty winds on mountain-slopes "sometimes shoot off a cannon." These explosive blasts touch only a short, narrow space, but in this they are almost irresistible.

Isolated clouds often soften and beautify the stern heights as they silently float and drift among peaks and passes. Flocks of these sky birds frequently float about together. On sunny days, in addition to giving a charm to the peaks, their restless shadows never tire of readjusting themselves and are ever trying to find a foundation or a place of rest upon the tempestuous topography of the heights below. Now and then a deep, dense cloud-stratum will cover the crests and envelop the summit slopes for days. These vapory strata usually feel but little wind and they vary in thickness from a few hundred to a few thousand feet. Sometimes one of these rests so serenely that it suggests an aggregation of clouds pushed off to one side because temporarily the sky does not need them elsewhere for either decorative or precipitative purposes. Now and then they do drop rain or snow, but most of the time they appear to be in a procrastinating mood and unable to decide whether to precipitate or to move on.

Commonly the upper surfaces of cloud-strata appear like a peaceful silver-gray sea. They appear woolly and sometimes fluffy, level, and often so vast that they sweep away beyond the horizon. Peaks and ridges often pierce their interminable surface with romantic continents and islands; along their romantic shores, above the surface of the picturesque sea, the airship could sail in safe poetic flight, though the foggy depths below were too dense for any traveler to penetrate.

One spring the snow fell continuously around my cabin for three days. Reports told that the storm was general over the Rocky Mountain region. Later investigations showed that that cloud and storm were spread over a quarter of a million square miles. Over this entire area there was made a comparatively even deposit of thirty inches of snow.

All over the area, the bottom, or under surface, of the cloud was at an altitude of approximately nine thousand feet. My cabin, with an altitude of nine thousand, was immersed in cloud, though at times it was one hundred feet or so below it. Fully satisfied of the widespread and general nature of the storm, and convinced of the comparatively level line of the bottom surface of the cloud, I determined to measure its vertical depth and observe its slow movements by climbing above its silver lining. This was the third day of the storm. On snowshoes up the mountainside I went through this almost opaque sheep's-wool cloud. It was not bitterly cold, but cloud and snow combined were blinding, and only a ravine and instinct enabled me to make my way.

At an altitude of about twelve thousand feet the depth of the snow became suddenly less, soon falling to only an inch or so. Within a few rods of where it began to grow shallow I burst through the upper surface of the cloud. Around me and above there was not a flake of snow. Over the entire storm-area of a quarter of a million square miles, all heights above twelve thousand had escaped both cloud and snow. The cloud, which thus lay between the altitudes of nine thousand and twelve thousand feet, was three thousand feet deep.

When I rose above the surface of this sea the sun was shining upon it. It was a smooth sea; not a breath of wind ruffled it. The top of Long's Peak rose bald and broken above. Climbing to the top of a commanding ridge, I long watched this beautiful expanse of cloud and could scarcely realize that it was steadily flinging multitudes of snowflakes upon slopes and snows below. Though practically stationary, this cloud expanse had some slight movements. These were somewhat akin to those of a huge raft that is becalmed in a quiet harbor. Slowly, easily, and almost imperceptibly the entire mass slid forward along the mountains; it moved but a short distance, paused for some minutes, then slowly slid back a trifle farther than it had advanced. After a brief stop the entire mass, as though anchored in the centre, started to swing in an easy, deliberate rotation; after a few degrees of movement it paused, hesitated, then swung with slow, heavy movement back. In addition to these shifting horizontal motions there was a short vertical one. The entire mass slowly sank and settled two or three hundred feet, then, with scarcely a pause, rose easily to the level from which it sank. Only once did it rise above this level.

During all seasons of the year there are oft-recurring periods when the mountains sit in sunshine and all the winds are still. In days of this kind the transcontinental passengers in glass-bottomed airships would have a bird's-eye view of sublime scenes. The purple forests, the embowered, peaceful parks, the drifted snows, the streams that fold and shine through the forests, — all these combine and cover magnificently the billowed and broken distances, while ever floating up from below are the soft, ebbing, and intermittent songs from white water that leaps in glory.

Though the summits of the Rocky Mountains are always cool, it is only in rare, brief times that they fall within the frigid spell of Farthest North and become cruelly cold. The climate among these mountain-tops is much milder than people far away imagine.

Mountain-Top Weather

The electrical effects that enliven and sometimes illuminate these summits are peculiar and often highly interesting. Thunderbolts — lightning-strokes — are rare, far less frequent than in most lowland districts. However, when lightning does strike the heights, it appears to have many times the force that is displayed in lowland strokes. My conclusions concerning the infrequency of thunderbolts on these sky-piercing peaks are drawn chiefly from my own experience. I have stood through storms upon more than a score of Rocky Mountain summits that were upward of fourteen thousand feet above the tides. Only one of these peaks was struck; this was Long's Peak, which rises to the height of 14,256 feet above the sea.

Seventy storms I have experienced on the summit of this peak, and during these it was struck but three times to my knowledge. One of these strokes fell a thousand feet below the top; two struck the same spot on the edge of the summit. The rock struck was granite, and the effects of the strokes were similar; hundreds of pounds of shattered rock fragments were flung horizontally afar. Out of scores of experiences in rain-drenched passes I have record of but two thunderbolts. Both of these were heavy. In all these instances the thunderbolt descended at a time when the storm-cloud was a few hundred feet above the place struck.

During the greater number of high-altitude storms the cloud is in contact with the surface or but little removed from it. Never have I known the lightning to strike when the clouds were close to the surface or touching it. It is, however, common, during times of low-dragging clouds, for the surface air to be heavily charged with electrical fluid. This often is accompanied with strange effects. Prominent among these is a low pulsating hum or an intermittent *buz-z-z-z*, with now and then a sharp *zit-zit!* Sometimes accompanying, at other times only briefly breaking in, are subdued camp-fire cracklings and roarings. Falling snowflakes, during these times, are occasionally briefly luminous, like fireflies, the instant they touch the earth. Hair-pulling is the commonest effect that people experience in these sizzling electrical storms. There is a straightening of the hairs and apparently a sharp pull upon each. As John Muir has it, "You are sure to be lost in wonder and praise and every hair of your head will stand up and hum and sing like an enthusiastic congregation." Most people take very gravely their first experience of this kind; especially when accompanied, as it often is, with apparent near-by bee-buzzings and a purplish roll or halo around the head. During these times a sudden finger movement will produce a crackling snap or spark.

On rare occasions these interesting peculiarities become irritating and sometimes serious to one. In "A Watcher on the Heights," in "Wild Life on the Rockies," I have described a case of this kind. A few people suffer from a muscular cramp or spasm, and occasionally the muscles are so tensed that breathing becomes difficult and heart-action disturbed. I have never known an electrical storm to be fatal. Relief from the effects of such a storm may generally be had by lying between big stones or beneath shelving rocks. On one occasion I saw two ladies and four gentlemen lay dignity aside and obtain relief by jamming into a place barely large enough for two. In my own case, activity invariably intensified these effects; and the touching of steel or iron often had the same results. For some years a family resided upon the slope of Mt. Teller, at an altitude of twelve thousand feet. Commonly during storms the stove and pipe were charged with fluid so heavily that it was a case of hands off and let dinner wait, and sometimes spoil, until the heavens shut off the current.

The sustaining buoyancy of the air to aerial things decreases with altitude. In this "light" air some motor machinery is less efficient than it is in the lowlands. It is probable that aviators will always find the air around uplifted peaks much less serviceable than this element upon the surface of the sea. But known and unknown dangers in the air will be mastered, and ere long the dangers to those who take flight through the air will be no greater than the dangers to those who go down to the sea in ships. Flying across the crest of the continent, above

Mountain-Top Weather

the crags and cañons, will be enchanting, and
this journey through the upper air may bring to
many the first stirring message from the rocks
and templed hills.

Rob of the Rockies

Rob of the Rockies

HURRYING out of the flood-swept mountains in northern Colorado, in May, 1905, I came upon a shaggy black and white dog, hopelessly fastened in an entanglement of flood-moored barbed-wire fence that had been caught in a clump of willows. He had been carried down with the flood and was coated with earth. Masses of mud clung here and there to his matted hair, and his handsome tail was encased as though in a plaster cast. He was bruised, and the barbs had given him several cuts. One ear was slit, and a blood-clot from a cut on his head almost closed his left eye.

Had I not chanced upon him, he probably would have perished from hunger and slow torture. Though he must have spent twelve hours in this miserable barbed binding, he made no outcry. The barbs repeatedly penetrated his skin, as I untangled and uncoiled the wires from around his neck and between his legs. As he neither flinched nor howled, I did him the injustice to suppose that he was almost dead. He trusted me, and as I rolled him about, taking off that last thorny tangle, the slit ear, bloody muzzle, and muddy head could not hide from me an expression of gratitude in his intelligent face.

Returning from a camping-trip, and narrowly escaping drowning, too, I was a dirty vagabond myself. When the last wire dropped from the prisoner, he enthusiastically began to share his earth coating with me. He leaped up and half clasped me in his fore legs, at the same time wiping most of the mud off his head on one side of my face. Then he darted between my legs, racing about and occasionally leaping or flinging himself against me; each time he leaped, he twisted as he came up so that he struck me with his back, head, or side, and thus managed to transfer much of this fertile coat to me. He finally ended by giving several barks, and then racing to the near-by river for a drink and a bath. I, too, needed another cloudburst.

Just what kinds of dogs may have made his

mixed ancestry could not be told. Occasionally
I had a glimpse of a collie in him, but for all
practical purposes he was a shepherd, and he
frequently exhibited traits for which the shepherd is celebrated. I could never find out where
he came from. It may be that the flood separated him from his master's team; he may have
been washed away from one of the flooded
ranches; or he may have been, as the stage-
driver later told me, "a tramp dog that has
been seen in North Park, Cheyenne, and Greeley." Home he may have left; master he may
have lost; or tramp he may have been; but he
insisted on going with me, and after a kindly
though forceful protest, I gave in and told him
he might follow.

The flood had swept all bridges away, and I
was hurrying down the Poudre, hoping to find
a place to cross without being compelled to swim.
He followed, and kept close to my heels as I
wound in and out among flood débris and wil-
low-clumps. But I did not find a place that
appeared shallow.

As it was necessary to cross, I patted my

companion good-by, thinking he would not care to go farther, and waded in. He squatted by the water's edge and set up a howl. I stopped and explained to him that this was very bad crossing for an injured dog, and that we would better separate; but he only howled the more. He wanted to go with me, but was afraid to try alone.

Returning to the bank, I found a rope in the flood wreckage, tied this around his neck and waded in. He followed cheerfully, but swam with effort. When about half way across, and in the water up to my shoulders, I attached myself to a floating log lest the dog should weaken and need help. Within sixty or seventy feet of the desired bank we struck a stretch of swift, deep water, in which I was compelled to let the animal go and swim for the shore. My companion was swept down by the current, and the rope caught on a snag, entangling my legs so that I had to cut it or drown. The current swept poor doggie against some stranded wreckage in midstream. On this he climbed, while I struggled on to the bank.

Rob of the Rockies

I called to him to come on, but he only howled.
Again I called, patted my knees, made friendly
gesticulations, and did all I could think of to
encourage him. Finally, I told him that if he
would only start I would come part way and be
ready to help him if he got into trouble. But
he would not start. Not desiring the task of
returning for him through the cold, strong current, and feeling in a hurry, I started on. He
howled and then cried so piteously that I went
back and towed him safely ashore.

That night some good people of the ranch
house treated both of us kindly, and in the
morning they wanted to keep my companion.
I was willing that he should stay, for he would
have a good place, and I was bound for Denver,
where I feared some accident would befall him.
But he growled and ran away when the man
advanced to tie him. I started on afoot and he
joined me, insisting on following.

All the time he had been with me his only
thought appeared to be to stay with me. Game,
dogs, horses, and people he saw and passed with
expressionless face, except two or three times

when he imagined I was in danger; then he was instantly alert for my defense. When the stage overtook us, and stopped to let me in, he leaped in also, and squatted by the driver with such an air of importance that I half expected to see him take the lines and drive.

I lost him in my rush to make the train at the station. He could, of course, have kept with me had he been without fear, or if he had really so desired. As the train pulled out, I saw him start down-street with an air of unconscious confidence that told of wide experience. He was a tramp dog.

The next time I saw him was several months later, in Leadville, some two hundred miles from where he left me. Where, in the mean time, he may have rambled, what towns he may have visited, or what good days or troubles he may have had, I have no means of knowing.

I came walking into Leadville with snowshoes under my arm, from two weeks' snowshoeing and camping on the upper slopes of the Rockies. The ends of broken tree limbs had torn numerous right-angled triangles in my clothes, my soft hat was unduly slouchy, and fourteen nights' intimate association with a camp-fire, along with only an infrequent, indifferent contact with water, had made me a sight to behold, — for dogs, anyway. On the outskirts, one snarly cur noticed me and barked; in a few minutes at least a dozen dogs were closely following and making me unwelcome to their haunts. They grew bold with time, numbers, and closer inspection of me. They crowded unpleasantly close. Realizing that if one of them became courageous enough to make a snap at my legs, all might follow his example, I began to sidle out of the middle of the street, intending to leap a fence close by and take refuge in a house.

Before I could realize it, they were snapping right and left at me, and howling as they collided with the tail of a snowshoe which I used as a bayonet. We were close to the fence, I trying to find time to turn and leap over; but I was too busy, and, without assistance, it is probable that I should have been badly bitten.

Suddenly there was something like a football

mix-up at my feet, then followed a yelping of curs, with tucked tails dashing right and left to avoid the ferocious tackles of a shaggy black and white dog. It was Rob, who was delighted to see me, and whom I assured that he was most welcome.

He had been seen about Leadville for two or three months, and several persons had bits of information concerning him. All agreed that he had held aloof from other dogs, and that he quietly ignored the friendly greetings of all who made advances. He was not quarrelsome, but had nearly killed a bulldog that had attacked a boy. On one occasion, a braying burro so irritated him that he made a savage attack on the long-eared beast, and sent him pell-mell down the street, braying in a most excited manner.

The drivers of ore wagons reported that he occasionally followed them to and from the mines up the mountainside. At one livery-stable he was a frequent caller, and usually came in to have a drink; but no one knew where he ate or slept. One day a little mittened girl had left her sled, to play with him. He had responded in a most friendly manner, and had raced, jumped, circled, and barked; at last he had carried her slowly, proudly on his back.

I grew greatly interested in his biography, and wondered what could have shaped his life so strangely. In what kind of a home was his pretty puppyhood spent? Why was he so indifferent to dogs and people, and had he left or lost a master?

Early next spring, after vainly trying to follow the trail of explorer Pike, I struck out on a road that led me across the Wet Mountain valley up into Sangre de Cristo Mountains. When well up into the mountains, I saw a large dog walking slowly toward me, and at once recognized him as Rob. Although clean and well-fed, he held his head low and walked as though discouraged. The instant he scented me, however, he leaped forward and greeted me with many a wag, bark, and leap. He was one hundred miles from Leadville, and fully three hundred miles from the flood scene on the Poudre. He faced about and followed me up into the alpine heights, far beyond trail. We saw a number of deer and many mountain sheep; these he barely noticed, but a bear that we came upon he was most eager to fight.

The second night in the mountains, near Horne's Peak, we had an exciting time with a mountain lion. Coyotes howled during the evening, much to the dog's annoyance. It was a cold night, and, being without bedding, I had moved the fire and lain down upon the warm earth. The fire was at my feet, a crag rose above my head, and Rob was curled up against my back. A shrill, uncanny cry of the lion roused me after less than an hour's sleep. The dog was frightened and cuddled up close to my face. The lion was on a low terrace in the crag, not many yards distant. Having been much in the wilds alone and never having been attacked by lions, I had no fear of them; but none had ever been so audacious as this one. I began to think that perhaps it might be true that a lion would leap upon a dog boldly at night, even though the dog lay at the feet of his master. I kept close watch, threw stones at suspicious shadows on the cliff terraces, and maintained a blazing fire.

Rob of the Rockies

Long before sunrise we started down the mountain. Both Rob and I were hungry, and although we startled birds and rabbits, Rob paid not the least attention to them. At noon, on Madano Pass, I lay down for a sleep and used Rob for a pillow. This he evidently enjoyed, for he lay still with head stretched out and one eye open.

At mid-afternoon we met a sheep-herder who was carrying a club. I had seen this man elsewhere, and, on recognizing me as he came up, he waved his club by the way of expressing gladness. Rob misinterpreted this demonstration, and dragged me almost to the frightened herder before I could make him understand that this ragged, unwashed, club-carrying fellow had no ill wishes for me.

I had in mind to climb Sierra Blanca the following day, and hoped to spend the night in a ranch house on the northern slope of this great peak. Toward sundown Rob and I climbed through a pole fence and entered the ranch house-yard. Round a corner of the house came a boy racing on a willow switch pony. On seeing us, he stopped, relaxed his hold on the willow and started for Rob. How happily he ran, holding out both eager hands! The dog sprang playfully backward, and began to dodge and bark as the boy laughingly and repeatedly fell while trying to catch him. Just as I entered the house, Rob was trying to climb to the top of the fence after his new playmate.

That night Rob was agreeable with every one in the house, and even had a romp with the cat. These people wanted to keep him, and offered money and their best saddle-horse. I knew that with them he would have kind treatment to the day of his death. I wanted him, too, but I knew the weeks of mountain-exploring just before me would be too hard for him. "Rob is a free dog," I said, "and is, of his own choice, simply traveling with me as a companion. I cannot sell or give him away. I like him, but, if he wants to stay, it will be a pleasure to me to leave him."

The next morning every one was wondering whether Rob would go or stay. The dog had made up his mind. He watched me prepare to leave with keenest interest, but it was evident that he had planned to stay, and his boy friend was very happy. As I passed through the yard, these two were playing together; at the gate I called good-by, at which Rob paused, gave a few happy barks, and then raced away, to try to follow his mountain boy to the top of the old pole fence.

Sierra Blanca

Sierra Blanca

J WAS rambling alone on snowshoes, doing some winter observations in the alpine heights of the Sangre de Cristo range. It was miles to the nearest house. There was but little snow upon the mountains, and, for winter, the day was warm. I was thirsty, and a spring which burst forth among the fragments of petrified wood was more inviting than the water-bottle in my pocket. The water was cool and clear, tasteless and, to all appearances, pure.

As I rose from drinking, a deadly, all-gone feeling overcame me. After a few seconds of this, a violent and prolonged nausea came on. Evidently I had discovered a mineral spring! Perhaps it was arsenic, perhaps some other poison. Poison of some kind it must have been, and poisonous mineral springs are not unknown.

The sickness was very like seasickness, with a severe internal pain and a mental stimulus added. After a few minutes I partly recovered from these effects and set off sadly for the nearest house of which I had heard. This was eight or ten miles distant and I hoped to find it through the guidance of a crude map which a prospector had prepared for me. I had not before explored this mountainous section.

The gulches and ridges which descended the slope at right angles to my course gave me a rough sea which kept me stirred up. I advanced in tottering installments; a slow, short advance would be made on wobbly legs, then a heave-to, as pay for the advance gained.

Now and then there was smoothness, and I took an occasional look at severe Sierra Blanca now looming big before me. It was mostly bare and brown with a number of icy plates and ornaments shining in the sun.

At last in the evening light, from the top of a gigantic moraine, I looked down upon the river and a log ranch-house nestling in a grassy open bordered with clumps of spruces. An old lady and gentleman with real sympathy in their faces stood in the doorway and for a moment

SIERRA BLANCA IN WINTER

watched me, then hastened to help me from the pole fence to the door.

While giving them an incoherent account of my experience, I fell into a stupor, and although I had evidently much to say concerning drinking and apparently showed symptoms of too much drink, these old people did not think me drunk. Waking from a fantastic dream I heard, "Does he need any more sage tea?" The Western pioneers have faith in sage tea and many ascribe to it all the life-saving, life-extending qualities usually claimed for patent medicines. The following morning I was able to walk about, while my slightly bloated, bronzed face did not appear so badly. Altogether, I looked much better than I felt.

These good old people declared that they had not seen better days, but that they were living the simple life from choice. They loved the peace of this isolated mountain home and the companionship of the grand old peak. In the Central States the wife had been a professor in a State school, while the husband had been a State's Attorney.

The Spell of the Rockies

The nearest neighbor was four miles down-stream, and no one lived farther up the mountain. The nearest railroad station was seventy rough mountain-road miles away. It appeared best to hasten to Denver, but two days in a jarring wagon to reach the railroad seemed more than I could endure. I had not planned even to try for the top of Colorado's highest peak in midwinter, but the way across Sierra Blanca was shorter and probably much easier than the way around. Across the range, directly over the shoulder of Sierra Blanca, lay historic Fort Garland. It was only thirty miles away, and I determined to cross the range and reach it in time for the midnight train. On hearing this resolution the old people were at first astonished, but after a moment they felt that they at last knew who I was.

"You must be the Snow Man! Surely no one but he would try to do this in winter."

They, with scores of other upland-dwellers, had heard numerous and wild accounts of my lone, unarmed camping-trips and winter adventures in the mountain snows.

Sierra Blanca

The misgivings of the old gentleman concerning the wisdom of my move grew stronger when he perceived how weak I was, as we proceeded on mule-back up the slope of Sierra Blanca. The ice blocked us at timber-line, and in his parting handclasp I felt the hope and fear of a father who sees his son go away into the world. He appeared to realize that I was not only weak, but that at any moment I might collapse. He knew the heights were steep and stern, and that in the twenty-odd miles to Fort Garland there was neither house nor human being to help me. Apparently he hoped that at the last moment I would change my mind and turn back.

Up the northern side of the peak I made my way. Now and then it was necessary to cut a few steps in the ice-plated steeps. The shoulder of the peak across which I was to go was thirteen thousand feet above the sea, and in making the last climb to this it was necessary to choose between a precipitous ice-covered slope and an extremely steep rock-slide, — more correctly a rock glacier. I picked my way up this with the greatest caution. To start a rock avalanche would be easy, for the loose rocks lay insecure on a slope of perilous steepness. From time to time in resting I heard the entire mass settling, snarling, and grinding its way with glacier slowness down the steep.

Just beneath the shoulder the tilting steepness of this rocky débris showed all too well that the slightest provocation would set a grinding whirlpool of a stone river madly flowing. The expected at last happened when a boulder upon which I lightly leaped settled and then gave way. The rocks before made haste to get out of the way, while those behind began readjusting themselves. The liveliest of foot-work kept me on top of the now settling, hesitating, and inclined-to-roll boulder. There was nothing substantial upon which to leap.

Slowly the heavy boulder settled forward with a roll, now right, now left, with me on top trying to avoid being tumbled into the grinding mill hopper below. At last, on the left, a sliding mass of crushed, macadamized rock offered a possible means of escape. Not daring to risk thrusting a leg into this uncertain mass, I allowed myself to fall easily backwards until my body was almost horizontal, and then face upwards I threw myself off the boulder with all my strength. The rock gave a great plunge, and went bounding down the slope, sending the smaller stuff flying before at each contact with the earth.

Though completely relaxed, and with the snowshoes on my back acting as a buffer, the landing was something of a jolt. For a few seconds I lay limp and spread out, and drifted slowly along with the slow-sliding mass of macadam. When this came to rest, I rose up and with the greatest concern for my foundation, made my way upwards, and at last lay down to breathe and rest upon the solid granite shoulder of Sierra Blanca.

In ten hours the midnight train would be due in Fort Garland, and as the way was all downgrade, I hoped that my strength would hold out till I caught it. But, turning my eyes from the descent to the summit, I forgot the world below, and also my poison-weakened body. Suddenly I felt and knew only the charm and the call of the summit. There are times when Nature completely commands her citizens. A splendid landscape, sunset clouds, or a rainbow on a near-by mountain's slope, — by these one may be as completely charmed and made as completely captive as were those who heard the music of Orpheus' lyre. My youthful dream had been to scale peak after peak, and from the earthly spires to see the scenic world far below and far away. All this had come true, though of many trips into the sky and cloudland, none had been up to the bold heights of Blanca. Thinking that the poisoned water might take me from the list of those who seek good tidings in the heights, I suddenly determined to reach those wintry wonder-heights while yet I had the strength. I rose from relaxation, laid down my snowshoes, and started for the summit.

Blanca is a mountain with an enormous amount of material in it, — enough for a score of sizable peaks. Its battered head is nearly two thousand feet above its rugged shoulder. The sun sank slowly as I moved along a rocky skyline ridge and at last gained the summit.

Sierra Blanca

Beyond an infinite ocean of low, broken peaks, sank the sun. It was a wonderful sunset effect in that mountain-dotted, mountain-walled plain, the San Luis Valley. Mist-wreathed peaks rose from the plain, one side glowing in burning gold, the other bannered with black shadows. The low, ragged clouds dragged slanting shadows across the golden pale. A million slender silver threads were flung out in a measureless horizontal fan from the far-away sun. The sunset from the summit of Sierra Blanca was the grandest that I have ever seen. The prismatic brilliancy played on peak and cloud, then changed into purple, fading into misty gray, while the light of this strong mountain day slowly vanished in the infinite silence of a perfect mountain night.

Then came the serious business of getting down and off the rough slope and out of the inky woods before darkness took complete possession. After intense vigilance and effort for two hours, I emerged from the forest-robed slope and started across the easy, sloping plain beneath a million stars.

The Spell of the Rockies

The night was mild and still. Slowly, across the wide brown way, I made my course, guided by a low star that hung above Fort Garland. My strength ran low, and, in order to sustain it, I moved slowly, lying down and relaxing every few minutes. My mind was clear and strangely active. With pleasure I recalled in order the experiences of the day and the wonderful sunset with which it came triumphantly to a close. As I followed a straight line across the cactus-padded plains, I could not help wondering whether the Denver physicians would tell me that going up to see the sunset was a serious blunder, or a poison-eliminating triumph. However, the possibility of dying was a thought that never came.

At eleven o'clock, when instinctively and positively I felt that I had traveled far enough, I paused; but from Fort Garland neither sound nor light came to greet me in the silent, mysterious night. I might pass close to the low, dull adobes of this station without realizing its presence. So confident was I that I had gone far enough that I commenced a series of constantly enlarging semicircles, trying to locate in the darkness the hidden fort. In the midst of these, a coyote challenged, and a dog answered. I hastened toward the dog and came upon a single low adobe full of Mexicans who could not understand me. However, their soft accents awakened vivid memories in my mind, and distinctly my strangely stimulated brain took me back through fifteen years to the seedling orange groves in the land of to-morrow where I had lingered and learned to speak their tongue. An offer of five dollars for transportation to Fort Garland in time for the midnight train sent Mexicans flying in all directions as though I had hurled a bomb.

Two boys with an ancient, wobbling horse and buckboard landed me at the platform as the headlight-glare of my train swept across it. The big, good-natured conductor greeted me with "Here's the Snow Man again, — worse starved than ever!"

The Wealth of the Woods

The Wealth of the Woods

THE ancients told many wonderful legends concerning the tree, and claimed for it numerous extraordinary qualities. Modern experience is finding some of these legends to be almost literal truth, and increasing knowledge of the tree shows that it has many of those high qualities for which it was anciently revered. Though people no longer think of it as the Tree of Life, they are beginning to realize that the tree is what enables our race to make a living and to live comfortably and hopefully upon this beautiful world.

Camping among forests quickly gives one a home feeling for them and develops an appreciation of their value. How different American history might have been had Columbus discovered a treeless land! The American forests have largely contributed to the development of the country. The first settlers on the Atlantic coast felled and used the waiting trees for home-building; they also used wood for fuel, furniture, and fortifications. When trading-posts were established in the wilderness the axe was as essential as the gun. From Atlantic to Pacific the pioneers built their cabins of wood. As the country developed, wood continued to be indispensable; it was used in almost every industry, and to-day it has a more general use than ever.

Forests enrich us in many ways. One of these is through the supply of wood which they produce, — which they annually produce. Wood is one of the most useful materials used by man. Wood is the home-making material. It gives good cheer to a million hearthstones. How extensively it is used for tools, furniture, and vehicles, for mine timbers and railroad development! The living influences which forests exert, the environments which they create and maintain, are potent to enable man best to manage and control the earth, the air, and the water, so that these will give him the greatest service and do him the least damage.

Forests are water-distributors, and everywhere their presence tends to prevent both

SPANISH MOSS AT LAKE CHARLES, LOUISIANA

floods and extreme low water; they check evaporation and assist drainage; they create soil; they resist sudden changes of temperature; they break and temper the winds; they do sanitary work by taking impurities from the air; they shelter and furnish homes for millions of birds which destroy enormous numbers of weed-seed and injurious insects. Lastly, and possibly most important, forests make this earth comfortable and beautiful. Next to the soil, they are the most useful and helpful of Nature's agencies.

Forests are moderators of climate. They heat and cool slowly. Their slow response to change resists sudden changes, and, consequently, they mitigate the rudeness with which sudden changes are always accompanied. Sudden changes of temperature are often annoying and enervating to man, and frequently do severe damage to domestic plants and animals. They sometimes have what may be called an explosive effect upon the life-tissues of many plants and animals which man has domesticated and is producing for his benefit. Many plants have been domesticated and largely so specialized that they have been rendered less hardy. With good care, these plants are heavy producers, but, to have from them a premium harvest each year, they need the genial clime, the stimulating shelter, and the constant protection which only forests can supply. Closely allied to changes of temperature is the movement of the air. In the sea every peninsula is a breakwater: on land every grove is a windbreak. The effect of the violence of high winds on fruited orchards and fields of golden grain may be compared to the beatings of innumerable clubs. Hot waves and cold waves come like withering breaths of flame and frost to trees and plants. High winds may be mastered by the forest. The forest will make even the Storm King calm, and it will also soften, temper, and subdue the hottest or the coldest waves that blow. Forests may be placed so as to make every field a harbor.

The air is an invisible blotter that is constantly absorbing moisture. Its capacity to evaporate and absorb increases with rapidity of movement. Roughly, six times as much water is evaporated from a place that is swept

126

by a twenty-five-mile wind as from a place in the dead calm of the forest. The quantity of water evaporated within a forest or in its shelter is many times less than is evaporated from the soil in an exposed situation. This shelter and the consequent decreased evaporation may save a crop in a dry season. During seasons of scanty rainfall the crops often fail, probably not because sufficient water has not fallen, but because the thirsty winds have drawn from the soil so much moisture that the water-table in the soil is lowered below the reach of the roots of the growing plants.

In the arid West the extra-dry winds are insatiable. In many localities their annual capacity to absorb water is greater than the annual precipitation of water. In "dry-farming" localities, the central idea is to save all the water that Nature supplies, to prevent the moisture from evaporating, to protect it from the robber winds. Forests greatly check evaporation, and Professor L. G. Carpenter, the celebrated irrigation engineer, says that forests are absolutely necessary for the interests of irrigated agriculture. Considering the many influences of the forest that are beneficial to agriculture, it would seem as though ideal forest environments would be the best annual assurance that the crops of the field would not fail and that the soil would most generously respond to the seed-sower.

So well is man served in the distribution of the waters and the management of their movements by the forests, that forests seem almost to think. The forest is an eternal mediator between winds and gravity in their never-ending struggle for the possession of the waters. The forest seems to try to take the intermittent and ever-varying rainfall and send the collected waters in slow and steady stream back to the sea. It has marked success, and one may say it is only to the extent the forest succeeds in doing this that the waters become helpful to man. Possibly they may need assistance in this work. Anyway, so great is the evaporation on the mountains of the West that John Muir says, "Cut down the groves and the streams will vanish." Many investigators assert that only thirty per cent of the rainfall is returned by the rivers to the sea. Evaporation — winds — probably carry away the greater portion of the remainder. Afforestation has created springs and streams, not by increasing rainfall, although the forests may do this, but by saving the water that falls, — by checking evaporation. On some exposed watersheds the winds carry off as much as ninety per cent of the annual precipitation. It seems plain that wider, better forests would mean deeper, steadier streams. Forests not only check evaporation, but they store water and guard it from the greed of gravity. The forest gets the water into the ground where a brake is put upon the pull of gravity. Forest floors are covered with fluffy little rugs and pierced with countless tree-roots. So all-absorbing is the porous, rug-covered forest floor that most of the water that falls in the forest goes into the ground; a small percentage may run off on the surface, but the greater part settles into the earth and seeps slowly by subterranean drainage, till at last it bubbles out in a spring some distance away and below the place where the raindrops came to earth. The underground drainage, upon which the forest insists, is much slower and steadier than the surface drainage of a treeless place. The tendency of the forest is to take the water of the widely separated rainy days and dole it out daily to the streams. The forest may be described as a large, ever-leaking reservoir.

The forest is so large a reservoir that it rarely overflows, and seepage from it is so slow that it seldom goes dry. The presence of a forest on a watershed tends to give the stream which rises thereon its daily supply of water, whether it rains every day or not. By checking evaporation, the forest swells the volume of sea-going water in this stream, and thereby increases its water-power and makes it more useful as a deep waterway. Forests so regulate stream-flow that if all the watersheds were forested but few floods would occur. Forest-destruction has allowed many a flood to form and foam and to ruin a thousand homes. A deforested hillside may, in a single storm, loose the hoarded soil of a thousand years. Deforestation may result in filling a river-channel and in stopping boats a thousand miles downstream. By bringing forests to our aid, we may almost domesticate and control winds and waters!

One of the most important resources is soil, — the cream of the earth, the plant-food of the world. Scientists estimate that it takes nature ten thousand years to create a foot of soil. This heritage of ages, though so valuable and so slowly created, may speedily be washed away and lost. Forests help to anchor it and to hold it in productive places. Every tree stands upon an inverted basket of roots and rootlets. Rains may come and rains may go, but these roots hold the soil in place. The soil of forest-covered hillsides is reinforced and anchored with a web-work of the roots and rootlets of the forest. Assisting in the soil-anchorage is the accumulation of twigs and leaves, the litter rugs on the forest floor. These cover the soil, and protect it from both wind and water erosion. The roots and rugs not only hold soil, but add to the soil matter by catching and holding the trash, silt, dust, and sediment that is blown or washed into the forest. The forest also creates new soil, enriches the very land it is using. Trash on a forest floor absorbs nitrogenous matter from the air; every fallen leaf is a flake of a fertilizer; roots pry rocks apart, and this sets up chemical action. Acids given off by tree-roots dissolve even the rocks, and turn these to soil. A tree, unlike most plants, creates more soil than it consumes. In a forest the soil is steadily growing richer and deeper.

Birds are one of the resources of the country. They are the protectors, the winged watchmen, of the products which man needs. Birds are hearty eaters, and the food which they devour consists mostly of noxious weed-seed and injurious insects. Several species of birds feed freely upon caterpillars, moths, wood-lice, wood-borers, and other deadly tree-enemies. Most species of birds need the forest for shelter, a home, and a breeding-place; and, having the forest, they multiply and fly out into the fields and orchards, and wage a more persistent warfare even than the farmer upon the insistent and innumerable crop-injuring weeds, and also the swarms of insatiable crop-devouring insects.

The Wealth of the Woods

Birds work for us all the time, and board themselves most of the time. Birds are of inestimable value to agriculture, but many of these useful species need forest shelter. So to lose a forest means at the same time to lose the service of these birds.

The forest is a sanitary agent. It is constantly eliminating impurities from the earth and the air. Trees check, sweep, and filter from the air quantities of filthy, germ-laden dust. Their leaves absorb the poisonous gases from the air. Roots assist in drainage, and absorb impurities from the soil. Roots also give off acids, and these acids, together with the acids released by the fallen, decaying leaves, have a sterilizing effect upon the soil. Trees help to keep the earth sweet and clean, and water which comes from a forested watershed is likely to be pure. Many unsanitary areas have been redeemed and rendered healthy by tree-planting.

Numerous are the products and the influences of the trees. Many medicines for the sick-room are compounded wholly or in part from the bark, the fruit, the juices, or the leaves of trees.

Fruits and nuts are at least the poetry of the dining-table. One may say of trees what the French physician said of water: needed externally, internally, and eternally! United we stand, but divided we fall, is the history of peoples and forests. Forest-destruction seems to offer the speediest way by which a nation may go into decline or death. "Without forests" are two words that may be written upon the maps of most depopulated lands and declining nations.

When one who is acquainted with both history and natural history reads of a nation that "its forests are destroyed," he naturally pictures the train of evils that inevitably follow, — the waste and failure that will come without the presence of forests to prevent. He realizes that the ultimate condition to be expected in this land is a waste of desolate distances, arched with a gray, sad sky beneath which a few lonely ruins stand crumbling and pathetic in the desert's drifting sand.

The trees are our friends. As an agency for promoting and sustaining the general welfare, the forest stands preëminent. A nation which

The Wealth of the Woods

appreciates trees, which maintains sufficient forests, and these in the most serviceable places, may expect to enjoy regularly the richest of harvests; it will be a nation of homes and land that is comfortable, full of hope, and beautiful.

The Forest Fire

The Forest Fire

FOREST fires led me to abandon the most nearly ideal journey through the wilds I had ever embarked upon, but the conflagrations that took me aside filled a series of my days and nights with wild, fiery exhibitions and stirring experiences. It was early September and I had started southward along the crest of the continental divide of the Rocky Mountains in northern Colorado. All autumn was to be mine and upon this alpine skyline I was to saunter southward, possibly to the land of cactus and mirage. Not being commanded by either the calendar or the compass, no day was to be marred by hurrying. I was just to linger and read all the nature stories in the heights that I could comprehend or enjoy. From my starting-place, twelve thousand feet above the tides, miles of continental slopes could be seen that sent their streams east and west to the two far-off seas. With many a loitering advance, with many a glad going back, intense days were lived. After two great weeks I climbed off the treeless heights and went down into the woods to watch and learn the deadly and dramatic ways of forest fires.

This revolution in plans was brought about by the view from amid the broken granite on the summit of Long's Peak. Far below and far away the magnificent mountain distances reposed in the autumn sunshine. The dark crags, snowy summits, light-tipped peaks, bright lakes, purple forests traced with silver streams and groves of aspen, — all fused and faded away in the golden haze. But these splendid scenes were being blurred and blotted out by the smoke of a dozen or more forest fires.

Little realizing that for six weeks I was to hesitate on fire-threatened heights and hurry through smoke-filled forests, I took a good look at the destruction from afar and then hastened toward the nearest fire-front. This was a smoke-clouded blaze on the Rabbit-Ear Range that was storming its way eastward. In a few hours it would travel to the Grand River, which

A FOREST FIRE ON THE GRAND RIVER

flowed southward through a straight, mountain-walled valley that was about half a mile wide. Along the river, occupying about half the width of the valley, was a picturesque grassy avenue that stretched for miles between ragged forest-edges.

There was but little wind and, hoping to see the big game that the flames might drive into the open, I innocently took my stand in the centre of the grassy stretch directly before the fire. This great smoky fire-billow, as I viewed it from the heights while I was descending, was advancing with a formidable crooked front about three miles across. The left wing was more than a mile in advance of the active though lagging right one. As I afterward learned, the difference in speed of the two wings was caused chiefly by topography; the forest conditions were similar, but the left wing had for some time been burning up a slope while the right had traveled down one. Fire burns swiftly up a slope, but slowly down it. Set fire simultaneously to the top and the bottom of a forest on a steep slope and the blaze at the bottom will overrun at least nine-tenths of the area. Flame and the drafts that it creates sweep upward.

Upon a huge lava boulder in the grassy stretch I commanded a view of more than a mile of the forest-edge and was close to where a game trail came into it out of the fiery woods. On this burning forest-border a picturesque, unplanned wild-animal parade passed before me.

Scattered flakes of ashes were falling when a herd of elk led the exodus of wild folk from the fire-doomed forest. They came stringing out of the woods into the open, with both old and young going forward without confusion and as though headed for a definite place or pasture. They splashed through a beaver pond without stopping and continued their way up the river. There was no show of fear, no suggestion of retreat. They never looked back. Deer straggled out singly and in groups. It was plain that all were fleeing from danger, all were excitedly trying to get out of the way of something; and they did not appear to know where they were going. Apparently they gave more troubled attention to the roaring, the breath, and the movements of that fiery, mysterious monster than to the seeking of a place of permanent safety. In the grassy open, into which the smoke was beginning to drift and hang, the deer scattered and lingered. At each roar of the fire they turned hither and thither excitedly to look and listen. A flock of mountain sheep, in a long, narrow, closely pressed rank and led by an alert, aggressive bighorn, presented a fine appearance as it raced into the open. The admirable directness of these wild animals put them out of the category occupied by tame, "silly sheep." Without slackening pace they swept across the grassy valley in a straight line and vanished in the wooded slope beyond. Now and then a coyote appeared from somewhere and stopped for a time in the open among the deer; all these wise little wolves were a trifle nervous, but each had himself well in hand. Glimpses were had of two stealthy mountain lions, now leaping, now creeping, now swiftly fleeing.

Bears were the most matter-of-fact fellows in the exodus. Each loitered in the grass and occasionally looked toward the oncoming danger. Their actions showed curiosity and anger, but not alarm. Each duly took notice of the surrounding animals, and one old grizzly even struck viciously at a snarling coyote. Two black bear cubs, true to their nature, had a merry romp. Even these serious conditions could not make them solemn. Each tried to prevent the other from climbing a tree that stood alone in the open; around this tree they clinched, cuffed, and rolled about so merrily that the frightened wild folks were attracted and momentarily forgot their fears. The only birds seen were some grouse that whirred and sailed by on swift, definite wings; they were going somewhere.

With subdued and ever-varying roar the fire steadily advanced. It constantly threw off an upcurling, unbroken cloud of heavy smoke that hid the flames from view. Now and then a whirl of wind brought a shower of sparks together with bits of burning bark out over the open valley.

Just as the flames were reaching the margin

of the forest a great bank of black smoke curled forward and then appeared to fall into the grassy open. I had just a glimpse of a few fleeing animals, then all became hot, fiery, and dark. Red flames darted through swirling black smoke. It was stifling. Leaping into a beaver pond, I lowered my own sizzling temperature and that of my smoking clothes. The air was too hot and black for breathing; so I fled, floundering through the water, down Grand River.

A quarter of a mile took me beyond danger-line and gave me fresh air. Here the smoke ceased to settle to the earth, but extended in a light upcurling stratum a few yards above it. Through this smoke the sunlight came so changed that everything around was magically covered with a canvas of sepia or rich golden brown. I touched the burned spots on hands and face with real, though raw, balsam and then plunged into the burned-over district to explore the extensive ruins of the fire.

A prairie fire commonly consumes everything to the earth-line and leaves behind it only a black field. Rarely does a forest fire make so

clean a sweep; generally it burns away the
smaller limbs and the foliage, leaving the tree
standing all blackened and bristling. This fire,
like thousands of others, consumed the litter
carpet on the forest floor and the mossy covering
of the rocks; it ate the underbrush, devoured
the foliage, charred and burned the limbs, and
blackened the trunks. Behind was a dead forest in a desolate field, a territory with millions
of bristling, mutilated trees, a forest ruin impressively picturesque and pathetic. From a
commanding ridge I surveyed this ashen desert
and its multitude of upright figures all blurred
and lifeless; these stood everywhere, — in the
gulches, on the slopes, on the ridges against the
sky, — and they bristled in every vanishing
distance. Over the entire area only a few trees
escaped with their lives; these were isolated in
soggy glacier meadows or among rock fields and
probably were defended by friendly air-currents
when the fiery billow rolled over them.

When I entered the burn that afternoon the
fallen trees that the fire had found were in ashes,
the trees just killed were smoking, while the

standing dead trees were just beginning to burn freely. That night these scattered beacons strangely burned among the multitudinous dead. Close to my camp all through that night several of these fire columns showered sparks like a fountain, glowed and occasionally lighted up the scene with flaming torches. Weird and strange in the night were the groups of silhouetted figures in a shadow-dance between me and the flickering, heroic torches.

The greater part of the area burned over consisted of mountain-slopes and ridges that lay between the altitudes of nine thousand and eleven thousand feet. The forest was made up almost entirely of Engelmann and Douglas spruces, alpine fir, and flexilis pine. A majority of these trees were from fifteen to twenty-four inches in diameter, and those examined were two hundred and fourteen years of age. Over the greater extent of the burn the trees were tall and crowded, about two thousand to the acre. As the fire swept over about eighteen thousand acres, the number of trees that perished must have approximated thirty-six million.

The Spell of the Rockies

Fires make the Rocky Mountains still more rocky. This bald fact stuck out all through this burn and in dozens of others afterward visited. Most Rocky Mountain fires not only skin off the humus but so cut up the fleshy soil and so completely destroy the fibrous bindings that the elements quickly drag much of it from the bones and fling it down into the stream-channels. Down many summit slopes in these mountains, where the fires went to bed-rock, the snows and waters still scoot and scour. The fire damage to some of these steep slopes cannot be repaired for generations and even centuries. Meantime these disfigured places will support only a scattered growth of trees and sustain only a sparse population of animals.

In wandering about I found that the average thickness of humus — decayed vegetable matter — consumed by this fire was about five inches. The removal of even these few inches of covering had in many places exposed boulders and bed-rock. On many shallow-covered steeps the soil-anchoring roots were consumed and the productive heritage of ages was left to

The Forest Fire

be the early victim of eager running water and insatiable gravity.

Probably the part of this burn that was most completely devastated was a tract of four or five hundred acres in a zone a little below timberline. Here stood a heavy forest on solid rock in thirty-two inches of humus. The tree-roots burned with the humus, and down crashed the trees into the flames. The work of a thousand years was undone in a day!

The loss of animal life in this fire probably was not heavy; in five or six days of exploring I came upon fewer than three dozen fire victims of all kinds. Among the dead were groundhogs, bobcats, snowshoe rabbits, and a few grouse. Flying about the waste were crested jays, gray jays ("camp birds"), and magpies. Coyotes came early to search for the feast prepared by the fire.

During the second day's exploration on the burn, a grizzly bear and I came upon two roasted deer in the end of a gulch. I was first to arrive, so Mr. Grizzly remained at what may have been a respectful distance, restlessly watching me.

With his nearness and impolite stare I found it very embarrassing to eat alone. However, two days of fasting had prepared me for this primitive feast; and, knowing that bears were better than their reputation, I kept him waiting until I was served. On arising to go, I said, "Come, you may have the remainder; there is plenty of it."

The fire was followed by clear weather, and for days the light ash lay deep and undisturbed over the burn. One morning conditions changed and after a few preliminary whirlwinds a gusty gale set in. In a few minutes I felt and appeared as though just from an ash-barrel. The ashen dust-storm was blinding and choking, and I fled for the unburned heights. So blinding was the flying ash that I was unable to see; and, to make matters worse, the trees with fire-weakened foundations and limbs almost severed by flames commenced falling. The limbs were flung about in a perfectly reckless manner, while the falling trees took a fiendish delight in crashing down alongside me at the very moment that the storm was most blinding. Being without nerves and incidentally almost choked, I ignored the falling bodies and kept going.

Several times I rushed blindly against limb-points and was rudely thrust aside; and finally I came near walking off into space from the edge of a crag. After this I sought temporary refuge to the leeward of a boulder, with the hope that the weakened trees would speedily fall and end the danger from that source. The ash flew thicker than ever did gale-blown desert dust; it was impossible to see and so nearly impossible to breathe that I was quickly driven forth. I have been in many dangers, but this is the only instance in which I was ever irritated by Nature's blind forces. At last I made my escape from them.

From clear though wind-swept heights I long watched the burned area surrender its slowly accumulated, rich store of plant-food to the insatiable and all-sweeping wind. By morning, when the wind abated, the garnered fertility and phosphates of generations were gone, and the sun cast the shadows of millions of leafless trees upon rock bones and barren earth. And the waters were still to take their toll.

The Spell of the Rockies

Of course Nature would at once commence to repair and would again upbuild upon the foundations left by the fire; such, however, were the climatic and geological conditions that improving changes would come but slowly. In a century only a good beginning could be made. For years the greater portion of the burn would be uninhabitable by bird or beast; those driven forth by this fire would seek home and food in the neighboring territory, where this influx of population would compel interesting readjustments and create bitter strife between the old wild-folk population and the new.

This fire originated from a camp-fire which a hunting-party had left burning; it lived three weeks and extended eastward from the starting-place. Along most of its course it burned to the timber-line on the left, while rocky ridges, glacier meadows, and rock fields stopped its extension and determined the side line on the right; it ran out of the forest and stopped in the grassy Grand River Valley. Across its course were a number of rocky ridges and grassy gorges where the fire could have been easily stopped by removing the scattered trees, — by burning the frail bridges that enabled the fire to travel from one dense forest to abundant fuel beyond. In a city it is common to smother a fire with water or acid, but with a forest fire usually it is best to break its inflammable line of communication by removing from before it a width of fibrous material. The axe, rake, hoe, and shovel are the usual fire-fighting tools.

A few yards away from the spot where the fire started I found, freshly cut in the bark of an aspen, the inscription: —

J S M

YALE 18

A bullet had obliterated the two right-hand figures.

For days I wandered over the mountains, going from fire to smoke and studying burns new and old. One comparatively level tract had been fireswept in 1791. On this the soil was good. Lodge-pole pine had promptly restocked the burn, but these trees were now being smothered out by a promising growth of Engelmann spruce.

The Spell of the Rockies

Fifty-seven years before my visit a fire had burned over about four thousand acres and was brought to a stand by a lake, a rocky ridge, and a wide fire-line that a snowslide had cleared through the woods. The surface of the burn was coarse, disintegrated granite and sloped toward the west, where it was exposed to prevailing high westerly winds. A few kinnikinnick rugs apparently were the only green things upon the surface, and only a close examination revealed a few stunted trees starting. It was almost barren. Erosion was still active; there were no roots to bind the finer particles together or to anchor them in place. One of the most striking features of the entire burn was that the trees killed by the fire fifty-seven years ago were standing where they died. They had excellent root-anchorage in the shattered surface, and many of them probably would remain erect for years. The fire that killed them had been a hot one, and it had burned away most of the limbs, and had so thoroughly boiled the pitch through the exterior of the trunk that the wood was in an excellent state of preservation.

A YELLOW PINE, FORTY-SEVEN YEARS AFTER IT
HAD BEEN KILLED BY FIRE

The Forest Fire

Another old burn visited was a small one in an Engelmann spruce forest on a moderate northern slope. It had been stopped while burning in very inflammable timber. It is probable that on this occasion either a rain or snow had saved the surrounding forest. The regrowth had slowly extended from the margin of the forest to the centre of the burn until it was restocked.

One morning I noticed two small fires a few miles down the mountain and went to examine them. Both were two days old, and both had started from unextinguished camp-fires. One had burned over about an acre and the other about four times that area. If the smaller had not been built against an old snag it probably would have gone out within a few hours after the congressman who built it moved camp. It was wind-sheltered and the blaze had traveled slowly in all directions and burned a ragged circle that was about sixty feet across.

The outline of the other blaze was that of a flattened ellipse, like the orbit of many a wandering comet in the sky. This had gone before the wind, and the windward end of its orbit closely encircled the place of origin. The camp-fire nucleus of this blaze had also been built in the wrong place, — against a fallen log which lay in a deep bed of decaying needles.

Of course each departing camper should put out his camp-fire. However, a camp-fire built on a humus-covered forest floor, or by a log, or against a dead tree, is one that is very difficult to extinguish. With the best of intentions one may deluge such a fire with water without destroying its potency. A fire thus secreted appears, like a lie, to have a spark of immortality in it.

A fire should not be built in contact with substances that will burn, for such fuel will prolong the fire's life and may lead it far into the forest. There is but little danger to the forest from a fire that is built upon rock, earth, sand, or gravel. A fire so built is isolated and it usually dies an early natural death. Such a fire — one built in a safe and sane place — is easily extinguished.

The larger of these two incipient fires was burning quietly, and that night I camped within its orbit. Toward morning the wind began to blow, this slow-burning surface fire began to leap, and before long it was a crown fire, traveling rapidly among the tree-tops. It swiftly expanded into an enormous delta of flame. At noon I looked back and down upon it from a mountain-top, and it had advanced about three miles into a primeval forest sea, giving off more smoke than a volcano.

I went a day's journey and met a big fire that was coming aggressively forward against the wind. It was burning a crowded, stunted growth of forest that stood in a deep litter carpet. The smoke, which flowed freely from it, was distinctly ashen green; this expanded and maintained in the sky a smoky sheet that was several miles in length.

Before the fire lay a square mile or so of old burn which was covered with a crowded growth of lodge-pole pine that stood in a deep, criss-crossed entanglement of fallen fire-killed timber. A thousand or more of these long, broken dead trees covered each acre with wreckage, and in this stood upward of five thousand live young ones. This would make an intensely hot and flame-writhing fire. It appears that a veteran spruce forest had occupied this burn prior to the fire. The fire had occurred fifty-seven years before. Trees old and young testified to the date. In the margin of the living forest on the edge of the burn were numerous trees that were fire-scarred fifty-seven years before; the regrowth on the burn was an even-aged fifty-six-year growth.

That night, as the fire neared the young tree growth, I scaled a rock ledge to watch it. Before me, and between the fire and the rocks, stood several veteran lodge-pole pines in a mass of dead-and-down timber. Each of these trees had an outline like that of a plump Lombardy poplar. They perished in the most spectacular manner. Blazing, wind-blown bark set fire to the fallen timber around their feet; this fire, together with the close, oncoming fire-front, so heated the needles on the lodge-poles that they gave off a smoky gas; this was issuing from every top when a rippling rill of purplish flame ran up one of the trunks. Instantly there was a flash and white flames flared upward more than one hundred feet, stood gushing for a few seconds, and then went out completely. The other trees in close succession followed and flashed up like giant geysers discharging flame. This discharge was brief, but it was followed by every needle on the trees glowing and changing to white incandescence, then vanishing. In a minute these leafless lodge-poles were black and dead.

The fire-front struck and crossed the lodge-pole thicket in a flash; each tree flared up like a fountain of gas and in a moment a deep, ragged-edged lake of flame heaved high into the dark, indifferent night. A general fire of the dead-and-down timber followed, and the smelter heat of this cut the green trees down, the flames widely, splendidly illuminating the surrounding mountains and changing a cloud-filled sky to convulsed, burning lava.

Not a tree was left standing, and every log went to ashes. The burn was as completely cleared as a fireswept prairie; in places there were holes in the earth where tree-roots had burned out. This burn was an ideal place for another lodge-pole growth, and three years later these pines were growing thereon as thick as wheat in a field. In a boggy area within the burn an acre or two of aspen sprang up; this area, however, was much smaller than the one that the fire removed from the bog. Aspens commonly hold territory and extend their holdings by sprouting from roots; but over the greater portion of the bog the fire had either baked or burned the roots, and this small aspen area marked the wetter part of the bog, that in which the roots had survived.

After destroying the lodge-pole growth the fire passed on, and the following day it burned away as a quiet surface fire through a forest of scattered trees. It crept slowly forward, with a yellow blaze only a few inches high. Here and there this reddened over a pile of cone-scales that had been left by a squirrel, or blazed up in a pile of broken limbs or a fallen tree-top; it consumed the litter mulch and fertility of the forest floor, but seriously burned only a few trees.

Advancing along the blaze, I came upon a veteran yellow pine that had received a large pot-hole burn in its instep. As the Western yellow pine is the best fire-fighter in the conifer family, it was puzzling to account for this deep burn. On the Rocky Mountains are to be found many picturesque yellow pines that have a dozen times triumphed over the greatest enemy of the forest. Once past youth, these trees possess a thick, corky, asbestos-like bark that defies the average fire. Close to this injured old fellow was a rock ledge that formed an influential part of its environment; its sloping surface shed water and fertility upon its feet; cones, twigs, and trash had also slid down this and formed an inflammable pile which, in burning, had bored into its ankle. An examination of its annual rings in the burned hole revealed the fact that it too had been slightly burned fifty-seven years before. How long would it be until it was again injured by fire or until some one again read its records?

Until recently a forest fire continued until stopped by rain or snow, or until it came to the edge of the forest. I have notes on a forest fire that lived a fluctuating life of four months. Once a fire invades an old forest, it is impossible speedily to get rid of it. "It never goes out," declared an old trapper. The fire will crawl into a slow-burning log, burrow down into a root, or eat its way beneath a bed of needles, and give off no sign of its presence. In places such as these it will hibernate for weeks, despite rain or snow, and finally some day come forth as ferocious as ever.

About twenty-four hours after the lodge-pole blaze a snow-storm came to extinguish the surface fire. Two feet of snow — more than three inches of water — fell. During the storm I was comfortable beneath a shelving rock, with a fire in front; here I had a meal of wild raspberries and pine-nuts and reflected concerning the uses of forests, and wished that every one might better understand and feel the injustice and the enormous loss caused by forest fires.

During the last fifty years the majority of the Western forest fires have been set by unextinguished camp-fires, while the majority of the others were the result of some human carelessness. The number of preventable forest fires

The Forest Fire

is but little less than the total number. True, lightning does occasionally set a forest on fire; I have personal knowledge of a number of such fires, but I have never known lightning to set fire to a green tree. Remove the tall dead trees from forests, and the lightning will lose the greater part of its kindling.

In forest protection, the rivers, ridge-tops, rocky gulches, rock-fields, lake-shores, meadows, and other natural fire-resisting boundary lines between forests are beginning to be used and can be more fully utilized for fire-lines, fire-fighting, and fire-defying places. These natural fire-barriers may be connected by barren cleared lanes through the forest, so that a fire-break will isolate or run entirely around any natural division of forest. With such a barrier a fire could be kept within a given section or shut out of it.

In order to fight fire in a forest it must be made accessible by means of roads and trails; these should run on or alongside the fire-barrier so as to facilitate the movements of fire patrols or fire-fighters. There should be with every forest an organized force of men who are eternally vigilant to prevent or to fight forest fires. Fires should be fought while young and small, before they are beyond control.

There should be crows'-nests on commanding crags and in each of these should be a lookout to watch constantly for starting fires or suspicious smoke in the surrounding sea of forest. The lookout should have telephonic connection with rangers down the slopes. In our national forests incidents like the following are beginning to occur: Upon a summit is stationed a ranger who has two hundred thousand acres of forest to patrol with his eyes. One morning a smudgy spot appears upon the purple forest sea about fifteen miles to the northwest. The lookout gazes for a moment through his glass and, although not certain as to what it is, decides to get the distance with the range-finder. At that instant, however, the wind acts upon the smudge and shows that a fire exists and reveals its position. A ranger, through a telephone at the forks of the trail below, hears from the heights, "Small fire one mile south of Mirror

164

The Forest Fire

Lake, between Spruce Fork and Bear Pass Trail, close to O'Brien's Spring." In less than an hour a ranger leaps from his panting pony and with shovel and axe hastily digs a narrow trench through the vegetable mould in a circle around the fire. Then a few shovelfuls of sand go upon the liveliest blaze and the fire is under control. As soon as there lives a good, sympathetic public sentiment concerning the forest, it will be comparatively easy to prevent most forest fires from starting and to extinguish those that do start.

With the snow over, I started for the scene of the first fire, and on the way noticed how much more rapidly the snow melted in the open than in a forest. The autumn sun was warm, and at the end of the first day most of the snow in open or fireswept places was gone, though on the forest floor the slushy, compacted snow still retained the greater portion of its original moisture. On the flame-cleared slopes there was heavy erosion; the fire had destroyed the root-anchorage of the surface and consumed the trash that would ordinarily have absorbed and delayed the water running off; but this, unchecked, had carried off with it tons of earthy material. One slope on the first burn suffered heavily; a part of this day's "wash" was deposited in a beaver pond, of half an acre, which was filled to the depth of three feet. The beavers, finding their subterranean exits filled with wash, had escaped by tearing a hole in the top of their house.

Leaving this place, I walked across the range to look at a fire that was burning beyond the bounds of the snowfall. It was in a heavily forested cove and was rapidly undoing the constructive work of centuries. This cove was a horseshoe-shaped one and apparently would hold the fire within its rocky ridges. While following along one of these ridges, I came to a narrow, tree-dotted pass, the only break in the confining rocky barrier. As I looked at the fire down in the cove, it was plain that with a high wind the fire would storm this pass and break into a heavily forested alpine realm beyond. In one day two men with axes could have made this pass impregnable to the assaults of any fire, no matter how swift the wind ally; but men were not then defending our forests and an ill wind was blowing.

Many factors help to determine the speed of these fires, and a number of observations showed that under average conditions a fire burned down a slope at about one mile an hour; on the level it traveled from two to eight miles an hour, while up a slope it made from eight to twelve. For short distances fires occasionally roared along at a speed of fifty or sixty miles an hour and made a terrible gale of flames.

I hurried up into the alpine realm and after half an hour scaled a promontory and looked back to the pass. A great cloud of smoke was streaming up just beyond and after a minute tattered sheets of flame were shooting high above it. Presently a tornado of smoke and flame surged into the pass and for some seconds nothing could be seen. As this cleared, a succession of tongues and sheets of flame tried to reach over into the forest on the other side of the pass, but finally gave it up. Just as I was beginning to feel that the forest around me was safe, a smoke-column arose among the trees by the pass. Probably during the first assault of the flames a fiery dart had been hurled across the pass.

Up the shallow forested valley below me came the flames, an inverted Niagara of red and yellow, with flying spray of black. It sent forward a succession of short-lived whirlwinds that went to pieces explosively, hurling sparks and blazing bark far and high. During one of its wilder displays the fire rolled forward, an enormous horizontal whirl of flame, and then, with thunder and roar, the molten flames swept upward into a wall of fire; this tore to pieces, collapsed, and fell forward in fiery disappearing clouds. With amazing quickness the splendid hanging garden on the terraced heights was crushed and blackened. By my promontory went this magnificent zigzag surging front of flame, blowing the heavens full of sparks and smoke and flinging enormous fiery rockets. Swift and slow, loud and low, swelling and vanishing, it sang its eloquent death song.

A heavy stratum of tarlike smoke formed

above the fire as it toned down. Presently this black stratum was uplifted near the centre and then pierced with a stupendous geyser of yellow flame, which reddened as it fused and tore through the tarry smoke and then gushed astonishingly high above.

A year or two prior to the fire a snow slide from the heights had smashed down into the forest. More than ten thousand trees were mowed, raked, and piled in one mountainous mass of wreckage upon some crags and in a narrow-throated gulch between them. This woodpile made the geyser flames and a bonfire to startle even the giants. While I was trying to account for this extraordinary display, there came a series of explosions in rapid succession, ending in a violent crashing one. An ominous, elemental silence followed. All alone I had enjoyed the surprises, the threatening uncertainties, and the dangerous experiences that swiftly came with the fire-line battles of this long, smoky war; but when those awful explosions came I for a time wished that some one were with me. Had there been, I should have turned and asked, while getting a better grip on my nerves, "What on earth is that?" While the startled mountain-walls were still shuddering with the shock, an enormous agitated column of steam shot several hundred feet upward where the fiery geyser had flamed. Unable to account for these strange demonstrations, I early made my way through heat and smoke to the big bonfire. In the bottom of the gulch, beneath the bonfire, flowed a small stream; just above the bonfire this stream had been temporarily dammed by fire wreckage. On being released, the accumulated waters thus gathered had rushed down upon the red-hot rocks and cliffs and produced these explosions.

In the morning light this hanging terraced garden of yesterday's forest glory was a stupendous charcoal drawing of desolation.

Insects in the Forest

Insects in the Forest

THE big trees of California are never attacked by insects. This immunity is extraordinary and may be the chief characteristic that enables these noble trees to live so long. Unfortunately it is not shared by other species. The American forests are infested with thousands of species of injurious and destructive insects. These insects, like the forest fires, annually kill numerous forest areas, and in addition leave millions of deformed and sickly trees scattered through the living forest to impair and imperil it. After some general tree studies which have occupied odd times for years and extended through the groves and forests of every State and Territory in the Union, the conclusion has been forced upon me that the forests are more widely wasted by insects than by fire.

Some of Nature's strange ways are exhibited in the interrelation of insects and fires in tree-killing. It is common for the attack of one of

these tree-enemies to open the way for the depredations of the other. The trees that insects
kill quickly become dry and inflammable and
ready kindling for the forest fire. On the other
hand, the injuries that green trees often receive
from forest fires render them most susceptible to
the attacks of insects.

This interrelation — almost coöperation —
between these arch-enemies of the forest was
impressed upon me during my early tree studies. One day I enjoyed a splendid forest sea
from the summit of a granite crag that pierced
this purple expanse. Near the crag a few clumps
of trees stood out conspicuous in robes of sear
yellow brown. Unable to account for this color-
ing of their needles, I went down and looked
them over. The trees had recently been killed
by insects. They were Western yellow pine,
and their needles, changed to greenish yellow,
still clung to them. In each clump of these pines
there were several stunted or deformed trees,
or trees that showed a recent injury. The
stunted and injured trees in these clumps were
attacked and killed by beetles the summer be-

fore my visit. In these injured trees the beetles had multiplied, and they emerged the following summer and made a deadly attack upon the surrounding vigorous trees. Although this latter attack was made only a month or two before my arrival, the trees were already dead and their needles had changed to a sickly greenish yellow. Amid one of these clumps was a veteran yellow pine that lightning had injured a few years before. Beetles attacked and killed this old pine about a year before I appeared upon the scene. It was the only tree in this now dead clump that was attacked on that first occasion; but some weeks before my visit the beetles in multiplied numbers swarmed forth from it and speedily killed the sound neighboring trees.

These conclusions were gathered from the condition of the trees themselves together with a knowledge of beetle habits. Not a beetle could be found in the lightning-injured pine, and its needles were dry and yellow. The near-by dead pines were full of beetles and their eggs; the needles, of a greenish yellow, were slightly tough and still contained a little sap.

The Spell of the Rockies

While I was in camp one evening, in the midst of these tree studies, the veteran pine, now dead, was again struck by lightning. As everything was drenched with rain, there appeared to be no likelihood of fire. However, the following morning the old pine was ablaze. In extinguishing the fire I found that it had started at the base of the tree at a point where the bolt had descended and entered the earth. At this place there was an accumulation of bark-bits from the trunk, together with fallen twigs and needles from the dead tree-top. Thus a dead, inflammable tree in the woods is kindling which at any moment may become a torch and set fire to the surrounding green forest. Although fires frequently sweep through and destroy a green forest, they commonly have their start among dead trees or trash.

The pine beetle just mentioned attacks and burrows into trees for the purpose of laying its eggs therein. When few in number they confine their attacks to trees of low vitality, — those that will easily succumb to their attack. The speedy death of the tree and the resultant chemical change in its sap appear to be necessary for the well-being of the deposited eggs or the youngsters that emerge from them. When these beetles are numerous they freely attack and easily kill the most vigorous of trees.

The pine beetle is one of a dozen species of bark beetles that are grouped under a name that means "killer of trees." Each year they kill many acres of forest, and almost every year some one depredation extends over several thousand acres. The way of each species is similar to that of the others. The beetles of each species vary in length from a tenth to a fifth of an inch. They migrate in midsummer, at the time of the principal attack. Swarming over the tree, they at once bore into and through the bark. Here short transverse or vertical galleries are run, and in these the eggs are laid.

In a short time the eggs hatch into grubs, and these at once start to feed upon the inner bark at right angles to the galleries, extending to right and left around the tree. It does not require many of them to girdle the tree. Commonly the tree is dead in two months or less.

All these little animals remain in the tree until late spring or early summer, when they emerge in multiplied swarms and repeat the deadly work in other trees.

The depredations of these insects are enormous. During the early eighties the Southern pine beetle ruined several thousand acres of pines in Texas. Ten years later, 1890–92, it swarmed through western North Carolina, Virginia, and West Virginia to southern Pennsylvania and over an area aggregating seventy-five thousand square miles, and killed pines of all species and ages, leaving but few alive. Within the past few years the mountain and Western pine beetles have ruined a one-hundred-thousand-acre lodge-pole pine tract in northeastern Oregon, destroying not less than ninety per cent of the stand. During the past decade the Black Hills beetle has been active over the Rocky Mountains, where in some districts it has destroyed from ten to eighty per cent of the Western yellow pines. In the Black Hills the forests over several thousand square miles are ruined.

These bug-killed trees deteriorate rapidly. In

Insects in the Forest

most cases a beetle-killed pine is pretty well rotted in five years and usually falls to pieces in less than a decade. Borers attack upon the heels of the beetles, and the holes made by the beetles admit water and fungi into the wood. This rapidly reduces the wood to a punky, rotten mass.

One day in Colorado I tore a number of wind-wrecked, bug-killed trees to pieces and was busily engaged examining the numerous population of grubs and borers, when some robins and other birds discovered the feast, collected, and impatiently awaited their turn. Perceiving the situation, I dragged a fragment of a log to one side for examination while the birds assembled to banquet and dispute.

Returning to the rotten logs for another grub-filled fragment, I paused to watch some wasps that, like the birds, were feasting upon these grubs. A wasp on finding a grub simply thrust his snout into the grub and then braced himself firmly as he bored down and proceeded to suck his victim's fluids. In throwing a log to one side I disturbed a bevy of slender banqueters that I had not seen. Instantly a number of wasps were effervescing round my head. Despite busy arms, they effectively peppered my face, and I fled to a neighboring brook to bathe my wounds.

While I was at a safe distance, cogitating as to the wisdom of returning for further examination of the logs, a black bear appeared down the opening. From his actions I realized that he had scented not myself but the feast in the log-pile. After sniffling, pointing, and tip-toeing, he lumbered toward the logs. Of course I was curious as to the manner of his reception and allowed him to go unwarned to the feast. Two Rocky Mountain jays gave a low, indifferent call on his approach, but the other birds ignored his coming. With his fore paw he tore a log apart and deftly picked up a number of grubs. All went well until he climbed upon the pile of wreckage and rolled a broken log off the top. This disturbed another wasp feast. Suddenly he grabbed his nose with both fore paws and tumbled off the pile. For a few seconds he was slapping and battling at a lively pace; then, with a *woof-f-f-f!* he fled — straight at me. I made a tangential move.

Insects in the Forest

The hardwoods are also warred upon by bugs, weevils, borers, and fungi. The percentage of swift deaths, however, that the insects cause among the hardwoods is much smaller than that among the pines; but the percentage of diseased and slow-dying hardwoods is much greater. The methods of beetles that attack oaks, hickories, aspens, and birches are similar to the methods of those that attack pines and spruces. They attack in swarms, bore through the bark, and deposit their eggs either in the inner bark or in the cambium, — the vitals of the tree. The grubs, on hatching, begin to feed upon the tree's vitals. In this feeding each grub commonly drives a minute tunnel from one to several inches in length. Where scores of grubs hatch side by side they drive a score of closely parallel tunnels. Commonly these are either horizontal or vertical and generally they are numerous enough to make many complete girdles around the tree. Girdling means cutting off the circulation, and this produces quick death.

While these beetles are busy killing unnumbered millions of trees annually, the various species of another group of beetles known as weevils are active in deforming and injuring even a greater number. They mutilate and deform trees by the millions. The work of the white-pine weevil is particularly devilish. It deposits its eggs in the vigorous shoots of the white-pine sapling. The eggs hatch, and the grubs feed upon and kill the shoot. Another shoot bursts forth to take the place of the one killed; this is attacked and either killed or injured. The result is a stunted, crooked, and much-forked tree.

Borers attack trees both old and young of many species, and a few of these species with wholesale deadly effect. Birches by the million annually fall a prey to these tree-tunnelers, and their deadly work has almost wiped the black locust out of existence. Borers pierce and honeycomb the tree-trunk. If their work is not fatal, it is speedily extended and made so by the fungi and rot that its holes admit into the tree.

Trees, like people, often entertain a number of troubles at once and have misfortunes in series. A seedling injured by one insect is more likely to be attacked again, and by some other insect, than is the sound seedling by its side. Let a seedling be injured, and relays of insects — often several species at a time and each species with a way of its own — will attack it through the seedling, sapling, pole, tree, and veteran stages of its growth until it succumbs. Or let a vigorous tree meet with an accident, and like an injured deer it becomes food for an enemy. If lightning, wind, or sleet split the bark or break a limb, through these wounds some spore or borer will speedily reach the tree's vitals. In many cases the deadly work of parasitic plants and fungi is interrelated with, and almost inseparable from, the destructive operations of predacious insects. Many so-called tree diseases are but the spread of rot and fungi through the wood by means of an entrance bored by a borer, weevil, or beetle.

The bark of a tree, like the skin on one's body, is an impervious, elastic armor that protects blood and tissues from the poisonous or corrupting touch or seizure of thousands of deadly and incessantly clamoring germs. Tear the skin on one's body or the bark upon a tree, and eternally vigilant microbes at once sow the wound with the seeds of destruction or decay. A single thoughtless stroke of an axe in the bark of a tree may admit germs that will produce a kind of blood-poisoning and cause slow death.

The false-tinder fungus apparently can spread and do damage only as it is admitted into the tree through insect-holes or the wounds of accidents. Yet its annual damage is almost beyond computation. This rot is widely distributed and affects a large number of species. As with insects, its outbreaks often occur and extend over wide areas upon which its depredations are almost complete. As almost all trees are susceptible to this punk-producer, it will not be easy to suppress.

The study of forest insects has not progressed far enough to enable one to make more than a rough approximation of the number of the important species that attack our common trees. However, more than five hundred species are known to afflict the sturdy oak, while four hun-

A TREE KILLED BY MISTLETOE AND BEETLES

Insects in the Forest

dred prey upon the bending willow. The birches supply food to about three hundred of these predacious fellows, while poplars feed and shelter almost as many. The pines and spruces are compelled permanently to pension or provide for about three hundred families of sucking, chewing parasites.

The recent ravages of the chestnut-tree blight and the appalling depredations of the gypsy and brown-tailed moths, together with other evils, suggest at once the bigness of these problems and the importance of their study and solution. The insect army is as innumerable as the leaves in the forest. This army occupies points of vantage in every part of the tree zone, has an insatiable appetite, is eternally vigilant for invasion, and is eager to multiply. It maintains incessant warfare against the forest, and every tree that matures must run a gantlet of enemies in series, each species of which is armed with weapons long specialized for the tree's destruction. Some trees escape unscarred, though countless numbers are killed and multitudes maimed, which for a time live almost useless

185

lives, ever ready to spread insects and disease among the healthy trees.

Every part of the tree suffers; even its roots are cut to pieces and consumed. Caterpillars, grubs, and beetles specialize on defoliation and feed upon the leaves, the lungs of the trees. The partial defoliation of the tree is devitalizing, and the loss of all its leaves commonly kills it. Not only is the tree itself attacked but also its efforts toward reproduction. The dainty bloom is food for a number of insect beasts, while the seed is fed upon and made an egg-depository by other enemies. Weevils, blight, gall, ants, aphids, and lice prey upon it. The seed drops upon the earth into another army that is hungry and waiting to devour it. The moment it sprouts it is gnawed, stung, bitten, and bored by ever-active fiends.

Many forest trees are scarred in the base by ground fires. These trees are entered by insects through the scars and become sources of rot and insect infection. Although these trees may for a time live on, it is with a rotten heart or as a mere hollow shell. A forest fire that sweeps raging through the tree-tops has a very different effect: the twigs and bark are burned off and the pitches are boiled through the exterior of the trunk and the wood fortified against all sources of decay. This preservative treatment often gives long endurance to fire-killed timber, especially when the trees killed are yellow pine or Douglas spruce. Many a night in the Rocky Mountains my eager, blazing camp-fire was burning timber that forest fires had killed forty and even sixty years before.

In forest protection and improvement the insect factor is one that will not easily down. Controlling the depredations of beetles, borers, weevils, and fungi calls for work of magnitude, but work that insures success. This work consists of the constant removal of both the infected trees and the dwarfed or injured ones that are susceptible to infection. Most forest insects multiply with amazing rapidity; some mother bark-beetles may have half a million descendants in less than two years. Thus efforts for the control of insect outbreaks should begin at once, — in the early stages of their activity. A single infested tree may in a year or two spread destruction through thousands of acres of forest.

Most insects have enemies to bite them. The ichneumon-fly spreads death among injurious grubs. Efforts to control forest-enemies will embrace the giving of aid and comfort to those insects that prey upon them. Bugs will be hunted with bugs. Already the gypsy moth in the East is being fought in this way. Many species of birds feed freely upon weevils, borers, and beetles. Of these birds, the woodpeckers are the most important. They must be protected and encouraged.

There are other methods of fighting the enemy. A striking and successful device for putting an end to the spruce-destroying beetle is to hack-girdle a spruce here and there in the forest at a season when the physiological make-up of the tree will cause it to change into a condition most favorable for the attraction of beetles. Like carrion, this changed condition appears to be scented from all quarters and afar. Swarms of beetles concentrate their attack upon this tree and bury themselves in it and deposit their eggs.

Insects in the Forest

The multiplied army will remain in the tree until late spring. Thus months of time may be had to cut and burn the tree, with its myriads of murderous guests. The freedom of the big trees from insect attacks suggests that man as well as nature may develop or breed species of trees that will better resist or even defy insects.

Insects are now damaging our forests to the extent of not less than one hundred million dollars annually. This we believe to be a conservative estimate. Yet these figures only begin to tell the story of loss. They tell only the commercial value of the timber. The other greater and higher values cannot be resolved into figures. Forest influences and forest scenes add much to existence and bestow blessings upon life that cannot be measured by gold.

Dr. Woodpecker, Tree-Surgeon

Dr. Woodpecker, Tree-Surgeon

ALTHOUGH the eagle has the emblematic place of honor in the United States, the downy woodpecker is distinguished as the most useful bird citizen. Of the eight hundred and three kinds of birds in North America, his services are most helpful to man. He destroys destructive forest insects. Long ago Nature selected the woodpecker to be the chief caretaker — the physician and surgeon — of the tree world. This is a stupendous task. Forests are extensive and are formed of hundreds of species of trees. The American woodpeckers have the supervision of uncounted acres that are forested with more than six hundred kinds of trees.

With the exception of the California big tree, each tree species is preyed upon by scores, and many species by hundreds, of injurious and deadly insects. Five hundred kinds of insects are known to prey upon the oak, and a complete count may show a thousand kinds. Many of these insects multiply with amazing rapidity, and at all times countless numbers of these aggressive pests form warrior armies with which the woodpecker must constantly contend.

In this incessant struggle with insects the woodpecker has helpful assistance from many other bird families. Though the woodpecker gives general attention to hundreds of kinds of insects, he specializes on those which injure the tree internally, — which require a surgical operation to obtain. He is a distinguished specialist; the instruments for tree-surgery are intrusted to his keeping, and with these he each year performs innumerable successful surgical operations upon our friends the trees.

Woodpeckers are as widely distributed as forests, — just how many to the square mile no one knows. Some localities are blessed with a goodly number, made up of representatives from three or four of our twenty-four woodpecker species. Forest, shade, and orchard trees receive their impartial attention. The annual saving from their service is enormous. Although this cannot be estimated, it can hardly be overstated.

A single borer may kill a tree; so, too, may a few beetles; while a small number of weevils will injure and stunt a tree so that it is left an easy victim for other insects. Borers, beetles, and weevils are among the worst enemies of trees. They multiply with astounding rapidity and annually kill millions of scattered trees. Annually, too, there are numerous outbreaks of beetles, whose depredations extend over hundreds and occasionally over thousands of acres. Caterpillars, moths, and saw-flies are exceedingly injurious tree-pests, but they damage the outer parts of the tree. Both they and their eggs are easily accessible to many kinds of birds, including the woodpeckers; but borers, beetles, and weevils live and deposit their eggs in the very vitals of the tree. In the tree's vitals, protected by a heavy barrier of wood or bark, they are secure from the beaks and claws of all birds except Dr. Woodpecker, the chief surgeon of the forest. About the only opportunity that other birds have to feed upon borers and beetles is during the brief time they occupy in emerging from the tree that they have killed, in their flight to some live tree, and during their brief exposure while boring into it.

Beetles live and move in swarms, and, according to their numbers, concentrate their attack upon a single tree or upon many trees. Most beetles are one of a dozen species of *Dendroctonus*, which means "tree-killer." Left in undisturbed possession of a tree, many mother beetles may have half a million descendants in a single season. Fortunately for the forest, Dr. Woodpecker, during his ceaseless round of inspection and service, generally discovers infested trees. If one woodpecker is not equal to the situation, many are concentrated at this insect-breeding place; and here they remain until the last dweller in darkness is reached and devoured. Thus most beetle outbreaks are prevented. Now and then all the conditions are favorable for the beetles, or the woodpecker may be persecuted and lose some of his family; so that, despite his utmost efforts, he fails to make the rounds of his forest, and the result is an outbreak of insects, with wide depredations. So important are these birds that the shooting of a single one may allow insects to multiply and waste acres of forest.

During the periods in which the insects are held in check the woodpecker ranges through the forest, inspecting tree after tree. Many times, during their tireless rounds of search and inspection, I have followed them for hours. On one occasion in the mountains of Colorado I followed a Batchelder woodpecker through a spruce forest all day long. Both of us had a busy day. He inspected eight hundred and twenty-seven trees, most of which were spruce or lodge-pole pine. Although he moved quickly, he was intensely concentrated, was systematic, and apparently did the inspection carefully. The forest was a healthy one and harbored only straggling insects. Now and then he picked up an isolated insect from a limb or took an egg-cluster from a break in the bark on a trunk. Only two pecking operations were required. On another occasion I watched a hairy woodpecker spend more than three days upon one tree-trunk; this he pecked full of holes and from its vitals he dragged more than a gross of devouring grubs. In this case not only was the beetle colony destroyed but the tree survived.

Woodpecker holes commonly are shallow, except in dead trees. Most of the burrowing or boring insects which infest living trees work in the outermost sapwood, just beneath the bark, or in the inner bark. Hence the doctor does not need to cut deeply. In most cases his peckings in the wood are so shallow that no scar or record is found. Hence a tree might be operated on by him a dozen times in a season, and still not show a scar when split or sawed into pieces. Most of his peckings simply penetrate the bark, and on living trees this epidermis scales off; thus in a short time all traces of his feast-getting are obliterated. I have, however, in dissecting and studying fallen trees, found a number of deep holes in their trunks which woodpeckers had made years before the trees came to their death. In one instance, as I have related in "The Story of a Thousand-Year Pine" in "Wild Life on the

WOODPECKER HOLES IN A PINE INJURED
BY LIGHTNING

Dr. Woodpecker, Tree-Surgeon

Rockies," a deep oblong hole was pecked in a pine nearly eight hundred years before it died. The hole filled with pitch and was overgrown with bark and wood.

Woodpeckers commonly nest in a dead limb or trunk, a number of feet from the ground. Here, in the heart of things, they excavate a moderately roomy nest. It is common for many woodpeckers to peck out a deep hole in a dead tree for individual shelter during the winter. Generally neither nest nor winter lodging is used longer than a season. The abandoned holes are welcomed as shelters and nesting-places by many birds that prefer wooden-walled houses but cannot themselves construct them. Chickadees and bluebirds often nest in them. Screech owls frequently philosophize within these retreats. On bitter cold nights these holes shelter and save birds of many species. One autumn day, while watching beneath a pine, I saw fifteen brown nuthatches issue from a woodpecker's hole in a dead limb. Just what they were doing inside I cannot imagine; the extraordinary number that had gathered therein made the incident so unusual that for a long time I hesitated to tell it. However, early one autumn, Mr. Frank M. Chapman climbed up the mountainside to see me, and, while resting on the way up, he beheld twenty-seven nuthatches emerge from a hole in a pine.

By tapping against dead tree-trunks I have often roused Mother Woodpecker from her nest. Thrusting out her head from a hole far above, she peered down with one eye and comically tilted her head to discover the cause of the disturbance. With long nose and head tilted to one side, she had both a storky and a philosophical appearance. The woodpecker, more than any other bird of my acquaintance, at times actually appears to need only a pair of spectacles upon his nose in order fully to complete his attitude and expression of wisdom.

The downy woodpecker, the smallest member of a family of twenty-four distinguished species, is the honored one. He is a confiding little fellow and I have often accompanied him on his daily rounds. He does not confine his attacks to the concealed enemies of the trees, but preys freely upon caterpillars and other enemies which feast upon their leaves and bloom. He appears most content close to the haunts of man and spends much of his time caring for orchards and cleaning up the shade trees. One morning in Missouri a downy alighted against the base of an apple tree within a few feet of where I was standing. He arrived with an undulating flight and swept in sideways toward the trunk, as though thrown. Spat! he struck. For a moment he stuck motionless, then he began to sidle round and up the trunk. Every now and then he tapped with his bill or else stopped to peer into a bark-cavity. He devoured an insect egg-cluster, a spider, and a beetle of some kind before ascending to the first limb.

Just below the point of a limb's attachment he edged about, giving the tree-trunk a rattling patter of taps with his bill. He was sounding for something. Presently a spot appeared to satisfy him. Adjusting himself, he rained blows with his pick-axe bill upon this, tilting his head and directing the strokes with an apparently automatic action, now and then giving a side swipe with his bill, probably to tear out a splinter or throw off a chip. In six minutes his prey was evidently in sight. Then he enlarged the hole and slightly deepened it vertically. Pausing, he thrust his head into the hole and his bill into a cavity beyond. With a backward tug he pulled his head out, then his bill, and at last his extended tongue with a grub impaled on its barbed point. This grub was dragged from the bottom of a crooked gallery at a point more than three inches beyond the bottom of the pecked hole. A useful bread-getting tool, this tongue of his, — a flexible, extensible spear.

In another tree he uncovered a feast of ants and their eggs. Once a grasshopper alighted against another tree-trunk up which he was climbing. Downy seized him instantly. In one tree-top he consumed an entire tent-caterpillar colony. In four hours he examined the trunks, larger limbs, and many of the smaller ones of one hundred and thirty-eight apple trees. In this time he made twenty-two excavations, five of which were large ones. Among the insects devoured were beetles, ants, their eggs and their aphids, a grasshopper, a moth or two, and a colony of caterpillars. I followed him closely, and frequently was within a few feet of him. Often I saw his eyes, or rather one eye at a time; and a number of times I imagined him about to look round and with merry laugh fly away, for he frequently acted like a happy child who is closely watching you while all the time merrily pretending not to see you. Yet, in all those four hours, he did not do a single thing which showed that he knew of my nearness or even of my existence!

Examining each tree in turn, he moved down a long row and at the end flew without the slightest pause to the first tree in the next row. From here he examined a line of trees diagonally across the orchard to the farther corner. Here he followed along the outside row until he flew away. The line of his inspection, from the time I first saw him until he flew away, formed a big letter "N."

During a wind-storm in a pine forest a dead tree fell near me and a flying limb knocked a downy, stunned, to the earth, by my feet. On reviving in my hands, he showed but little excitement, and when my hands opened he pushed himself off as though to dive to the earth; but he skimmed and swung upward, landing against a tree-trunk about twenty feet distant. Up this he at once began to skate and sidle, exploring away as though nothing had happened and I were only a stump.

Little Boy Grizzly

Little Boy Grizzly

ONE day, while wandering in the pine woods on the slope of Mt. Meeker, I came upon two young grizzly bears. Though they dodged about as lively as chickens, I at last cornered them in a penlike pocket of fallen trees.

Getting them into a sack was one of the liveliest experiences I ever had. Though small and almost starved, these little orphans proceeded to "chew me up" after the manner of big grizzlies, as is told of them in books. After an exciting chase and tussle, I would catch one and thrust him into the sack. In resisting, he would insert his claws into my clothes, or thrust them through the side of the sack; then, while I was trying to tear him loose, or to thrust him forcibly in, he would lay hold of a finger, or take a bite in my leg. Whenever he bit, I at once dropped him, and then all began over again.

Their mother had been killed a few days before I found them; so, of course, they were famished and in need of a home; but so bitterly did they resist my efforts that I barely succeeded in taking them. Though hardly so large as a collie when he is at his prettiest, they were nimble athletes.

At last I started home, the sack over my shoulder, with these lively *Ursus horribilis* in the bottom of it. Their final demonstration was not needed to convince me of the extraordinary power of their jaws. Nevertheless, while going down a steep slope, one managed to bite into my back through sack and clothes, so effectively that I responded with a yell. Then I fastened the sack at the end of a long pole, which I carried across my shoulder, and I was able to travel the remainder of the distance to my cabin without another attack in the rear.

Of course the youngsters did not need to be taught to eat. I simply pushed their noses down into a basin of milk, and the little red tongues at once began to ply; then raw eggs and bread were dropped into the basin. There was no hesitation between courses; they simply gobbled the food as long as I kept it before them.

Little Boy Grizzly

Jenny and Johnny were pets before sundown. Though both were alert, Johnny was the wiser and the more cheerful of the two. He took training as readily as a collie or shepherd-dog, and I have never seen any dog more playful. All bears are keen of wit, but he was the brightest one of the wild folk that I have ever known. He grew rapidly, and ate me almost out of supplies. We were intimate friends in less than a month, and I spent much time playing and talking with him. One of the first things I taught him was, when hungry, to stand erect with arms extended almost horizontally, with palms forward. I also taught him to greet me in this manner.

One day, after two weeks with me, he climbed to the top of a pole fence to which he was chained. Up there he had a great time; he perched, gazed here and there, pranced back and forth, and finally fell off. His chain tangled and caught. For a few seconds he dangled in the air by the neck, then slipped through his collar and galloped off up the mountainside and quickly disappeared in the woods. I supposed he was gone for good. Although I followed for several hours, I did not even catch sight of him.

This little boy had three days of runaway life, and then concluded to return. Hunger drove him back. I saw him coming and went to meet him; but kept out of sight until he was within twenty feet, then stepped into view. Apparently a confused or entangled mental condition followed my appearance. His first impulse was to let me know that he was hungry by standing erect and outstretching his arms; this he started hastily to do.

In the midst of this performance, it occurred to him that if he wanted anything to eat he must hurry to me; so he interrupted his first action, and started to carry his second into instant effect. These incomplete proceedings interrupted and tripped one another three or four times in rapid succession. Though he tumbled about in comic confusion while trying to do two things at once, it was apparent through all that his central idea was to get something to eat.

And this, as with all boys, was his central idea much of the time. I did not find anything

JOHNNY AND JENNY

that he would not eat. He simply gobbled scraps from the table, — mountain sage, rhubarb, dandelion, and apples. Of course, being a boy, he liked apples best of all.

If I approached him with meat and honey upon a plate and with an apple in my pocket, he would smell the apple and begin to dance before me, ignoring the eatables in sight. Instantly, on permission, he would clasp me with both fore paws and thrust his nose into the apple pocket. Often, standing between him and Jenny, I alternately fed each a bit. A few times I broke the regular order and gave Jenny two bits in succession. At this Johnny raged, and usually ended by striking desperately at me; I never flinched, and the wise little rogue made it a point each time to miss me by an inch or two. A few other people tried this irritating experiment with him, but he hit them every time. However, I early tried to prevent anything being done that teased or irritated him. Visitors did occasionally tease him, and frequently they fed the two on bad-temper-producing knickknacks.

Occasionally the two quarreled, but not more

frequently than two ordinary children; and these quarrels were largely traceable to fight-producing food mixtures. Anyway, bears will maintain a better disposition with a diet of putrid meat, snakes, mice, and weeds than upon desserts of human concoction.

Naturally bears are fun-loving and cheerful; they like to romp and play. Johnny played by the hour. Most of the time he was chained to a low, small shed that was built for his accommodation. Scores of times each day he covered all the territory that could be traversed while he was fastened with a twelve-foot chain. Often he skipped back and forth in a straight line for an hour or more. These were not the restless, aimless movements of the caged tiger, but those of playful, happy activity. It was a pleasure to watch this eager play; in it he would gallop to the outer limit of his chain, then, reversing his legs without turning his body, go backward with a queer, lively hippety-hop to the other end, then gallop forward again. He knew the length of his chain to an inch. No matter how wildly he rushed after some bone-stealing dog, he was never jerked off his feet by forgetting his limitations.

He and Scotch, my collie, were good friends and jolly playmates. In their favorite play Scotch tried to take a bone which Johnny guarded; this brought out from both a lively lot of feinting, dodging, grabbing, and striking. Occasionally they clinched, and when this ended, Johnny usually tried for a good bite or two on Scotch's shaggy tail. Scotch appeared always to have in mind that the end of Johnny's nose was sensitive, and he landed many a good slap on this spot.

Apparently, Johnny early appreciated the fact that I would not tease him, and also that I was a master who must be obeyed. One day, however, he met with a little mishap, misjudged things, and endeavored to make it lively for me. I had just got him to the point where he enjoyed a rocking-chair. In this chair he sat up like a little man. Sometimes his fore paws lay awkwardly in his lap, but more often each rested on an arm of the big chair. He found rocking such a delight that it was not long until he learned to rock himself. This brought on the mishap. He had grown over-confident, and one day was rocking with great enthusiasm. Suddenly, the big rocker, little man and all, went over backward. Though standing by, I was unable to save him, and did not move. Seeing his angry look when he struck the floor, and guessing his next move, I leaped upon the table. Up he sprang, and delivered a vicious blow that barely missed, but which knocked a piece out of my trousers.

Apparently no other large animal has such intense curiosity as the grizzly. An object in the distance, a scent, a sound, or a trail, may arouse this, and for a time overcome his intense and wary vigilance. In satisfying this curiosity he will do unexpected and apparently bold things. But the instant the mystery is solved he is himself again, and may run for dear life from some situation into which his curiosity has unwittingly drawn him. An unusual noise behind Johnny's shed would bring him out with a rush, to determine what it was. If not at once satisfied as to the cause, he would put his fore paws on the top of the shed and peer over in the most eager and inquiring manner imaginable. Like a scout, he spied mysterious and dim objects afar. If a man, a dog, or a horse, appeared in the distance, he quickly discovered the object, and at once stood erect, with fore paws drawn up, until he had a good look at it. The instant he made out what it was, he lost interest in it. At all times he was vigilant to know what was going on about him.

He was like a boy in his fondness for water. Usually, when unchained and given the freedom of the place, he would spend much of the time in the brook, rolling, playing, and wading. He and I had a few foot-races, and usually, in order to give me a better chance, we ran down hill. In a two-hundred-yard dash he usually paused three or four times and waited for me to catch up; and I was not a slow biped, either.

The grizzly, though apparently awkward and lumbering, is really one of the most agile of beasts. I constantly marveled at Johnny's lightness of touch, or the deftness of movement of his fore paws. With but one claw touching it, he could slide a coin back and forth on the floor more rapidly and lightly than I could. He would slide an eggshell swiftly along without breaking it. Yet by using but one paw, he could, without apparent effort, overturn rocks that were heavier than himself.

One day, while he slept in the yard, outstretched in the sun, I opened a large umbrella and put it over him, and waited near for him to wake up. By and by the sleepy eyes half opened, but without a move he closed them and slept again. Presently he was wide awake, making a quiet study of the strange thing over him, but except to roll his eyes, not a move did he make. Then a puff of wind gave sudden movement to the umbrella, rolling it over a point or two. At this he leaped to his feet, terribly frightened, and made a dash to escape this mysterious monster. But, as he jumped, the wind whirled the umbrella, and plump into it he landed. An instant of desperate clawing, and he shook off the wrecked umbrella and fled in terror. A minute or two later I found him standing behind the house, still frightened and trembling. When I came up and spoke to him, he made three or four lively attempts to bite my ankles. Plainly, he felt that I had played a mean and uncalled-for trick upon him. I talked to him for some time and endeavored to explain the matter to him.

A sudden movement of a new or mysterious object will usually frighten any animal. On more than one occasion people have taken advantage of this characteristic of wild beasts, and prevented an attack upon themselves. In one instance I unconsciously used it to my advantage. In the woods, one day, as I have related elsewhere, two wolves and myself unexpectedly met. With bared teeth they stood ready to leap upon me. Needing something to keep up my courage and divert my thoughts, it occurred to me to snap a picture of them. This effectively broke the spell, for when the kodak door flew open they wheeled and fled.

Autumn came, and I was to leave for a forestry tour. The only man that I could persuade to stay at my place for the winter was one who neither understood nor sympathized with my wide-awake and aggressive young grizzly. Realizing that the man and the bear would surely clash, and perhaps to the man's disadvantage, I settled things once and for all by sending Johnny to the Denver Zoo.

He was seven months old when we parted, and apparently as much attached to me as any dog to master. I frequently had news of him, but let two years go by before I allowed myself the pleasure of visiting him. He was lying on the ground asleep when I called, while around him a number of other bears were walking about. He was no longer a boy bear, but a big fellow. In my eagerness to see him I forgot to be cautious and, climbing to the top of the picket fence, leaped into the pen, calling, "Hello, Johnny!" as I leaped, and repeating this greeting as I landed on the ground beside him. He jumped up, fully awake, and at once recognized me. Instantly, he stood erect, with both arms extended, and gave a few happy grunts of joy and by way of greeting.

I talked to him for a little while and patted him as I talked. Then I caught a fore paw in my hand and we hopped and pranced about as in old times. A yell from the outside brought me to my senses. Instinctively I glanced about for a way of escape, though I really did not feel that I was in danger. We were, however, the observed of all observers, and I do not know which throng was staring with greater interest and astonishment, — the bears in the pen or the spectators on the outside.

Alone with a Landslide

Alone with a Landslide

REALIZING the importance of traveling as lightly as possible during my hasty trip through the Uncompahgre Mountains, I allowed myself to believe that the golden days would continue. Accordingly I set off with no bedding, with but little food, and without even snowshoes. A few miles up the trail, above Lake City, I met a prospector coming down and out of these mountains for the winter. "Yes," he said, "the first snow usually is a heavy one, and I am going out now for fear of being snowed-in for the winter." My imagination at once pictured the grand mountains deeply, splendidly covered with snow, myself by a camp-fire in a solemn primeval forest without food or bedding, a camp-bird on a near-by limb sympathizing with me in low, confiding tones, the snow waist-deep and mountains-wide. Then I dismissed the imaginary picture of winter and joyfully climbed the grand old mountains amid the low

223

and leafless aspens and the tall and richly robed firs.

I was impelled to try to make this mountain realm a National Forest and felt that sometime it would become a National Park. The wonderful reports of prospectors about the scenery of this region, together with what I knew of it from incomplete exploration, eloquently urged this course upon me. My plan was to make a series of photographs, from commanding heights and slopes, that would illustrate the forest wealth and the scenic grandeur of this wonderland. In the centre Uncompahgre Peak rose high, and by girdling it a little above the timber I obtained a number of the desired photographs, and then hurried from height to height, taking other pictures of towering summits or their slopes below that were black and purpling with impressive, pathless forests.

The second evening I went into camp among some picturesque trees upon a skyline at an altitude of eleven thousand feet above the tides. While gathering wood for a fire, I paused to watch the moon, a great globe of luminous gold, rise strangely, silently into the mellow haze of autumn night. For a moment on the horizon it paused to peep from behind a crag into a scattered group of weird storm-beaten trees on a ridge before me, then swiftly floated up into lonely, misty space. Just before I lay down for the night, I saw a cloud-form in the dim, low distance that was creeping up into my moonlit world of mountains. Other shadowy forms followed it. A little past midnight I was awakened by the rain falling gently, coldly upon my face. As I stood shivering with my back to the fire, there fell an occasional feathery flake of snow.

Had my snowshoes been with me, a different lot of experiences would have followed. With them I should have stayed in camp and watched the filmy flakes form their beautiful white feathery bog upon the earth, watched robes, rugs, and drapery decorate rocks and cliffs, or the fir trees come out in pointed, spearhead caps, or the festoons form upon the limbs of dead and lifeless trees, — crumbling tree-ruins in the midst of growing forest life. To be without food or snowshoes in faraway mountain snows is about as serious as to be adrift in a lifeboat without food or oars in the ocean's wide waste. In a few minutes the large, almost pelt-like flakes were falling thick and fast. Hastily I put the two kodaks and the treasured films into water-tight cases, pocketed my only food, a handful of raisins, adjusted hatchet and barometer, then started across the strange, snowy mountains through the night.

The nearest and apparently the speediest way out lay across the mountains to Ridgway; the first half of this fifteen miles was through a rough section that was new to me. After the lapse of several years this night expedition appears a serious one, though at the time it gave me no concern that I recall. How I ever managed to go through that black, storm-filled night without breaking my neck amid the innumerable opportunities for accident, is a thing that I cannot explain.

I descended a steep, rugged slope for a thousand feet or more with my eyes useless in the eager falling of mingled rain and snow. Nothing could be seen, but despite slow, careful going a dead limb occasionally prodded me. With the deliberation of a blind man I descended the long, steep, broken, slippery slope, into the bottom of a cañon. Now and then I came out upon a jumping-off place; here I felt before and below with a slender staff for a place to descend; occasionally no bottom could be found, and upon this report I would climb back a short distance and search out a way.

Activity kept me warm, although the cold rain drenched me and the slipperiness of slopes and ledges never allowed me to forget the law of falling bodies. At last a roaring torrent told me that I was at the bottom of a slope. Apparently I had come down by the very place where the stream contracted and dashed into a deep, narrow box cañon. Not being able to go down stream or make a crossing at this point, I turned and went up the stream for half a mile or so, where I crossed the swift, roaring water in inky darkness on a fallen Douglas spruce, — for such was the arrangement of its limbs and the feel of the wood in its barkless trunk, that these told me it was a spruce, though I could see nothing.

During this night journey I put myself both in feeling and in fact in a blind man's place, — the best lesson I ever had to develop deliberation and keenness of touch.

The next hour after crossing the stream I spent in climbing and descending a low wooded ridge with smooth surface and gentle slopes. Then there was one more river, the Little Cimarron, to cross. An Engelmann spruce, with scaly, flaky bark, that had stood perfectly perpendicular for a century or two but had recently been hurled to the horizontal, provided a long, vibrating bridge for me to cross on. Once across, I started to climb the most unstable mountain that I had ever trodden.

Mt. Coxcomb, up which I climbed, is not one of the "eternal hills" but a crumbling, dissolving, tumbling, transient mountain. Every hard rain dissolves, erodes, and uncovers the sides of this mountain as if it were composed of sugar, paste, and stones. It is made up of a confused mingling of parts and masses of soluble and flinty materials. Here change and erosion run riot after every rain. There is a great falling to

NEAR THE TOP OF MT. COXCOMB

pieces; gravity, the insatiable, is temporarily satisfied, and the gulches feast on earthy materials, while the river-channel is glutted with crushed cliffs, acres of earth, and the débris of ruined forests. Here and there these are flung together in fierce confusion.

On this bit of the wild world's stage are theatrical lightning changes of scenes, — changes that on most mountains would require ten thousand years or more. It is a place of strange and fleeting landscapes; the earth is ever changing like the sky. In wreathed clouds a great cliff is born, stands out bold and new in the sunshine and the blue. The Storm King comes, the thunders echo among crags and cañons, the broken clouds clear away, and the beautiful bow bends above a ruined cliff.

Here and there strange, immature monsters are struggling to rise, — to free themselves from the earth. Occasionally a crag is brought forth full grown during one operation of gravity, erosion, and storm, and left upon a foundation that would raise corn but never sustain cliff or crag. Scattered monoliths at times indulge in a contest of leaning the farthest from the perpendicular without falling. The potato-patch foundations of these in time give way, then gravity drags them head foremost, or in broken installments, down the slope.

Among the forested slopes that I traversed there were rock-slides, earthy glaciers, and leafless gulches with crumbling walls. Some of these gulches extended from bottom to top of the mountain, while others were digging their way. An occasional one had a temporary ending against the bottom of a kingly cliff, whose short reign was about to end as its igneous throne was disorganized and decomposed. The storm and darkness continued as I climbed the mountain of short-lived scenes, — a mountain so eagerly moving from its place in the sky to a bed in the sea. The saturation had softened and lubricated the surface; these sedimentary slopes had been made restless by the rain.

I endeavored to follow up one of the ridges, but it was narrow and all the pulpy places very slippery. Fearing to tumble off into the dark unknown, I climbed down into a gully and up this made my way toward the top. All my mountain experience told me to stay on the ridge and not travel in darkness the way in which gravity flings all his spoils.

The clouds were low, and I climbed well up into them. The temperature was cooler, and snow was whitening the earth. When I was well up to the silver lining of the clouds, a gust of wind momentarily rent them, and I stood amid snow-covered statuary, — leaning monoliths and shattered minarets all weird and enchanting in the moonlight. A few seconds later I was in darkness and snowstorm again.

The gulch steepened and apparently grew shallower. Occasionally a mass of mud or a few small stones rolled from the sides of the gulch to my feet and told that saturation was at work dissolving and loosening anchorages and foundations. It was time to get out of the gulch. While I was making haste to do so, there came a sudden tremor instantly followed by an awful crash and roar. Then *r-r-rip! z-zi-ip! s-w-w-r-r-ip!* A bombardment of flying, bounding, plunging rocks from an overturned cliff above was raking my gulch. Nothing could be seen, but several slaps in the face from dashes of snow which these rock missiles disturbed and displaced was expressively comprehensive.

As this brief bombardment ceased, the ominous sounds from above echoing among the cliffs shouted warning of an advancing landslide. This gave a little zest to my efforts to get out of the gulch; too much perhaps, for my scramble ended in a slip and a tumble back to the bottom. In the second attempt a long, uncovered tree-root reached down to me in the darkness, and with the aid of this I climbed out of the way of the avalanche. None too soon, however. With quarreling and subdued grinding sounds the rushing flood of landslide material went past, followed by an offensive smell.

While I paused listening to the monster groan and grind his way downward, the cliffs fired a few more rock missiles in my direction. One struck a crag beside me. The explosive contact gave forth a blast of sputtering sparks and an offensive, rotten-egg smell. A flying fragment of this shattered missile struck my left instep, breaking one of the small bones.

Fortunately my foot was resting in the mud when struck. When consciousness came back to me I was lying in the mud and snow, drenched, mud-bespattered, and cold. The rain and snow had almost ceased to fall, and while I was bandaging my foot the pale light of day began to show feebly through heavy clouds. If that luminous place is in the eastern horizon, then I have lost my sense of direction. An appeal to the compass brought no consolation, for it said laconically, "Yes, you are turned around now, even though you never were before." The accuracy of the compass was at once doubted, — but its decree was followed.

Slowly, painfully, the slippery, snowy steeps were scaled beneath a low, gloomy sky. My plan was to cross the north shoulder of Mt. Coxcomb and then down slope and gulch descend to the deeply filled alluvium Uncompahgre valley and the railroad village of Ridgway. With the summit only a few feet above, the wall became so steep and the hold so insecure that it appeared best to turn back lest I be precipitated from the cliff. The small, hard points in the sedimentary wall had been loosened in their settings by the rain. Climbing this wall with two good feet in a dry time would be adventurous pastime. While I was flattened against the wall, descending with greatest caution, there came a roaring crash together with a trembling of earth and air. An enormous section of the opposite side of the mass that I was on had fallen away, and the oscillations of the cliff nearly hurled me to the rock wreckage at the bottom of the wall.

On safe footing at last, I followed along the bottom of the summit cliff and encountered the place from which the rocks had been hurled at me in the darkness and where a cliff had fallen to start the slide. It was evident that the storm waters had wrecked the foundation of the cliff. Ridges and gullies of the Bad Land's type fluted the slope and prevented my traveling along close to the summit at right angles to the slope. There appeared no course for me but to descend to the Little Cimarron River. Hours were required for less than two miles of painful though intensely interesting travel.

It was a day of landslides, — just as there are, in the heights, days of snow slides. This excessive saturation after months of drought left cohesion and adhesion but slight hold on these strange sedimentary mixtures. The surface tore loose and crawled; cliffs tumbled. After counting the crash and echoing roar of forty-three fallen cliffs, I ceased counting and gave more attention to other demonstrations.

On the steeps, numerous fleshy areas crawled, slipped, and crept. The front of a long one had brought up against a rock ledge while the blind rear of the mass pressed powerfully forward, crumpling, folding, and piling the front part against the ledge. At one place an enormous rocky buttress had tumbled over. Below, the largest piece of this, a wreck in a mass of mud, floated slowly down the slope in a shallow, moderately tilted gulch. This buttress had been something of an impounding, retaining wall against which loosened, down-drifting materials had accumulated into a terrace. The terrace had long been adorned with a cluster of tall spruces whose presence produced vegetable mould and improved soil conditions.

On the falling-away of this buttress the tree-plumed terrace commenced to sag and settle. The soil-covered débris was well roped together and reinforced with tree-roots. When I came along, these tall trees, so long bravely erect, were leaning, drooping forward. Their entire foundation had slipped several feet and was steadily crowding out over the pit from which gravity had dragged the buttress. The trees, with their roots wedged in crevices, were anchored to bed-rock and clinging on for dear life. Now and then a low, thudding, earth-muffled sound told of strained or ruptured roots. The foundation steadily gave way while the trees drooped dangerously forward. United on the heights, the brave trees had struggled through the seasons, and united they would go down together. They had fixed and fertilized the spoil from the slopes above. This spoil had been held and made to produce, and prevented from going down to clog the channel of the Little Cimarron

or making with the waters the long, sifting, shifting journey, joining at last the lifeless soil deposits in the delta tongues of the Colorado. But
the steadfast trees, with all their power to check
erosion and create soil, were to fall before the
overwhelming elements.

Farther and farther the unsupported and
water-lubricated foundation slipped; more and
more the trees leaned and drooped forward; until
gravity tore all loose and plunged the trees head
foremost into the pit, crushing down upon tumbled tons of rocks, soil, matted mud, and roots,
— all the wreckage of the time-formed, tree-
crowned terrace.

The slide that narrowly missed me in the
night was a monster one and grew in magnitude
as it brutally rooted and gouged its way downward. After descending more than half a mile it
struck an enormous dome rock, which stayed
a small part of it, while the remainder, deflected,
made an awesome plunge and engulfed a small,
circular grove in an easily sloping grassy plot.
Most of the towering spruces were thrown down
and deeply buried beneath mud, smashed cliffs,

and the mangled forms of trees from up the slope. A few trees on the margin of the grove were left standing, but they suffered from cruel bruises and badly torn bark.

On the farther side of the grove a number of the trees were bent forward but only partly buried; with heads and shoulders out, they were struggling to extricate themselves, and now and then one shook an arm free from the débris. Over the place where a few hours before tall tree plumes had stood in the sky, a fierce confusion of slide wreckage settled and tumbled to pieces while the buried and half-buried trees whispered, murmured, and sighed as they struggled to rise.

Out with nature trees are supposed to stand in one place all their lives, but one of the most interesting movements of this elemental day was the transplanting, by gravity, of an entire clump of tall old firs. Water released these trees, and they appeared to enjoy being dragged by gravity to a new home and setting. I was resting my foot and watching a gigantic monolithic stone settle and come down gracefully, when a tree-clump on the skyline just beyond appeared to move forward several yards, then make a stop. While I was trying to decide whether they really had moved or not, they moved forward again with all their earthly claims, a few square rods of surface together with their foundations beneath. With all tops merrily erect they slid forward, swerving right and left along the line of least resistance, and finally came to rest in a small unclaimed flat in which no doubt they grew up with the country.

The many-sized slides of that weird day showed a change of position varying from a few feet to a mile. Several ploughed out into the Little Cimarron and piled its channel more than full of spoils from the slopes. Through this the river fought its way, and from it the waters flowed richly laden with earthy matter.

The great changes which took place on Mt. Coxcomb in a few hours were more marked and extensive than the alterations in most mountains since the Sphinx began to watch the shifting, changing sands by the Nile.

By mid-afternoon the air grew colder and the snow commenced to deepen upon the earth.

The Spell of the Rockies

Bedraggled and limping, I made slow progress down the slope. Just at twilight a mother bear and her two cubs met me. They probably were climbing up to winter-quarters. I stood still to let them pass. When a few yards distant the bear rose up and looked at me with a combination of curiosity, astonishment, and perhaps contempt. With *Woof! Woof!* more in a tone of disgust than of fear or anger, she rushed off, followed by the cubs, and the three disappeared in the darkening, snow-filling forest aisles.

The trees were snow-laden and dripping, but on and on I went. Years of training had given me great physical endurance, and this, along with a peculiar mental attitude that Nature had developed in me from being alone in her wild places at all seasons, gave me a rare trust in her and an enthusiastic though unconscious confidence in the ultimate success of whatever I attempted to accomplish out of doors.

About two o'clock in the morning I at last descended to the river. The fresh débris on my side of the stream so hampered traveling that it became necessary to cross. Not finding any fallen-tree bridge, I started to wade across in a wide place that I supposed to be shallow. Midway and hip-deep in the swift water, I struck the injured foot against a boulder, momentarily flinching, and the current swirled me off my feet. After much struggling and battling with the turbulent waters, I succeeded in reaching the opposite shore. This immersion did not make me any wetter than I was or than I had been for hours, but the water chilled me; so I hurried forward as rapidly as possible to warm up.

After a few steps the injured leg suddenly became helpless, and I tumbled down in the snow. Unable to revive the leg promptly and being very cold from my icy-water experience, I endeavored to start a fire. Everything was soaked and snow-covered; the snow was falling and the trees dripping water; I groped about on my hands and one knee, dragging the paralyzed leg; all these disadvantages, along with chattering teeth and numb fingers, made my fire-starting attempts a series of failures.

That night of raw, primitive life is worse in retrospect than was the real one. Still I was deadly in earnest at the time. Twenty-four hours of alertness and activity in the wilds, swimming and wading a torrent of ice-water at two o'clock in the morning, tumbling out into the wet, snowy wilds miles from food and shelter, a crushed foot and a helpless leg, the penetrating, clinging cold, and no fire, is going back to nature about ten thousand years farther than it is desirable to go. But I was not discouraged even for a moment, and it did not occur to me to complain, though, as I look back now, the theory of non-resistance appears to have been carried a trifle too far. At last the fire blazed. After two hours beside it I went down the river greatly improved. The snow was about fifteen inches deep.

Shortly before daylight I felt that I was close to a trail I had traveled, one that came to Cimarron near by Court-House Rock. Recrossing the river on a fallen log, I lay down to sleep beneath a shelving rock with a roaring fire before me, sleeping soundly and deeply until the crash of an overturned cliff awakened me. Jumping to my feet, I found the storm over with the

COURT-HOUSE ROCK

Alone with a Landslide

clouds broken and drifting back and forth in two strata as though undecided whether to go or remain. Above a low, lazy cloud, I caught a glimpse of Turret-Top, and turning, beheld Court-House Rock.

The foot gave no pain as I limped along the trail I had so often followed. Now and then I turned to take a photograph. The stars and the lights in the village were just appearing when I limped into the surgeon's office in Ridgway.

The Maker of Scenery and Soil

The Maker of Scenery and Soil

URING my first boyish exploring trip in the Rocky Mountains I was impressed with the stupendous changes which the upper slope of these mountains had undergone. In places were immense embankments and wild deltas of débris that plainly had come from elsewhere. In other places the rough edges of the cañons and ridges had been trimmed and polished; their cliffs and projections were gone and their surfaces had been swept clean of all loose material. Later, I tried vainly to account for some cañon walls being trimmed and polished at the bottom while their upper parts were jagged. In most cañons the height of the polishings above the bottom was equal on both walls, with the upper edge of the polish even or level for the entire length of the cañon. In one cañon, in both floor and walls, were deep lateral scratches in the rocks.

The Spell of the Rockies

One day I found some polished boulders perched like driftwood on the top of a polished rock dome; they were porphyry, while the dome was flawless granite. They plainly had come from somewhere else. How they managed to be where they were was too much for me. Mountain floods were terrible but not wild enough in their fiercest rushes to do this. Upon a mountainside across a gorge about two miles distant, and a thousand feet above the perched boulders on the dome, I found a porphyry outcrop; but this situation only added to my confusion. I did not then know of the glacial period, or the actions of glaciers. It was a delightful revelation when John Muir told me of these wonders.

Much of the earth's surface, together with most mountain-ranges, have gone through a glacial period or periods. There is extensive and varied evidence that the greater portion of the earth has been carved and extensively changed by the Ice King. Substantial works, blurred and broken records, and impressive ruins in wide array over the earth show long and active possession by the Ice King, as eloquently as the monumental ruins in the Seven Hills tell of their intense association with man.

Both the northern and the southern hemispheres have had their heavy, slow-going floods of ice that appear to have swept from the polar world far toward the equator. During the great glacial period, which may have lasted for ages, a mountainous flood of ice overspread America from the north and extended far down the Mississippi Valley. This ice may have been a mile or more in depth. It utterly changed the topography and made a new earth. Lakes were filled and new ones made. New landscapes were formed: mountains were rubbed down to plains, morainal hills were built upon plains, and streams were moved bodily.

It is probable that during the last ice age the location and course of both the Ohio and the Missouri Rivers were changed. Originally the Missouri flowed east and north, probably emptying into a lake that had possession of the Lake Superior territory. The Ice King deliberately shoved this river hundreds of miles toward the south. The Ohio probably had a similar experience. These rivers appear to mark the "Farthest South" of the ice; their position probably was determined by the ice. Had a line been traced on the map along the ragged edge and front of the glacier at its maximum extension, this line would almost answer for the present position of the Missouri and Ohio Rivers.

The most suggestive and revealing words concerning glaciers that I have ever read are these of John Muir in "The Mountains of California": "When we bear in mind that all the Sierra forests are young, growing upon moraine soil recently deposited, and that the flank of the range itself, with all its landscapes, is new-born, recently sculptured, and brought to light of day from beneath the ice mantle of the glacial winter, then a thousand lawless mysteries disappear and broad harmonies take their places."

"A glacier," says Judge Junius Henderson, in the best definition that I have heard, "is a body of ice originating in an area where the annual accumulation of snow exceeds the dissipation, and moving downward and outward to an area where dissipation exceeds accumulation."

THE HALLETT GLACIER

The Maker of Scenery and Soil

A glacier may move forward only a few feet in a year or it may move several feet in a day. It may be only a few hundred feet in length, or, as during the Ice Age, have an area of thousands of square miles. The Arapahoe Glacier moves slowly, as do all small glaciers and some large ones. One year's measured movement was 27.7 feet near the centre and 11.15 near the edge. This, too, is about the average for one year, and also an approximate movement for most small mountain glaciers. The centre of the glacier, meeting less resistance than the edges, commonly flows much more rapidly. The enormous Alaskan glaciers have a much more rapid flow, many moving forward five or more feet a day.

A glacier is the greatest of eroding agents. It wears away the surface over which it flows. It grinds mountains to dust, transports soil and boulders, scoops out lake-basins, gives flowing lines to landscapes. Beyond comprehension we are indebted to them for scenery and soil.

Glaciers, or ice rivers, make vast changes. Those in the Rocky Mountains overthrew cliffs, pinnacles, and rocky headlands. These in part were crushed and in part they became embedded in the front, bottom, and sides of the ice. This rock-set front tore into the sides and bottom of its channel — after it had made a channel! — with a terrible, rasping, crushing, and grinding effect, forced irresistibly forward by a pressure of untold millions of tons. Glaciers, large and small, the world over, have like characteristics and influences. To know one glacier will enable one to enjoy glaciers everywhere and to appreciate the stupendous influence they have had upon the surface of the earth.

They have planed down the surface and even reduced mountain-ridges to turtle outlines. In places the nose of the glacier was thrust with such enormous pressure against a mountainside that the ice was forced up the slope which it flowed across and then descended on the opposite side. Sustained by constant and measureless pressure, years of fearful and incessant application of this weighty, flowing, planing, ploughing sandpaper wore the mountain down. In time, too, the small ragged-edged, V-shaped ravines became widened, deepened, and extended into enormous U-shaped glaciated gorges.

Glaciers have gouged or scooped many basins in the solid rock. These commonly are made at the bottom of a deep slope where the descending ice bore heavily on the lever or against a reverse incline. The size of the basin thus made is determined by the size, width, and weight of the glacier and by other factors. In the Rocky Mountains these excavations vary in size from a few acres to a few thousand. They became lake-basins on the disappearance of the ice.

More than a thousand lakes of glacial origin dot the upper portions of the Rocky Mountains of Colorado. Most of these are above the altitude of nine thousand feet, and the largest, Grand Lake, is three miles in length. Landslides and silt have filled many of the old glacier lake basins, and these, overgrown with grass and sedge, are called glacier meadows.

Vast was the quantity of material picked up and transported by these glaciers. Mountains were moved piecemeal, and ground to boulders, pebbles, and rock-flour in the moving. In addition to the material which the glacier gathered up and excavated, it also carried the wreckage brought down by landslides and the eroded matter poured upon it by streams from the heights. Most of the material which falls upon the top of the upper end of the glacier ultimately works its way to the bottom, where, with the other gathered material, it is pressed against the bottom and sides and used as a cutting or grinding tool until worn to a powder or pebbles.

Train-loads of débris often accumulate upon the top of the glacier. On the lower course this often is a hundred feet or more above the surface, and as the glacier descends and shrivels, enormous quantities of this rocky débris fall off the sides and, in places, form enormous embankments; these often closely parallel long stretches of the glacier like river levees.

The large remainder of the material is carried to the end of the glacier, where the melting ice unloads and releases it. This accumulation, which corresponds to the delta of a river, is the terminal moraine. For years the bulk of the ice may melt away at about the same place; this accumulates an enormous amount of débris; an advance of the ice may plough through this and repile it, or the retreat of the ice or a changed direction of its flow may pile the débris elsewhere and over wide areas. Many of these terminal moraines are an array of broken embankments, small basin-like holes and smooth, level spaces. The débris of these moraines embraces rock-flour, gravel, pebbles, a few angular rock-masses, and enormous quantities of many-sized boulders, — rocks rounded by the grind of the glacial mill.

Strange freight, of unknown age, these creeping ice rivers bring down. One season the frozen carcass of a mountain sheep was taken from the ice at the end of the Arapahoe Glacier. If this sheep fell into a crevasse at the upper end of the glacier, its carcass probably had been in the ice for more than a century. Human victims, too, have been strangely handled by glaciers. It appears that in 1820 Dr. Hamil and a party of climbers were struck by a snowslide on the slope of Mont Blanc. One escaped with his life, while the others were swept down into a crevasse and buried so deeply in the snow and ice that their bodies could not be recovered. Scientists said that at the rate the glacier was moving it would give up its dead after forty years. Far down the mountain forty-one years afterward, the ice gave up its victims. A writer has founded on this incident an interesting story, in which the bodies are recovered in an excellent state of preservation, and an old woman with sunken cheeks and gray hair clasps the youthful body of her lover of long ago, the guide.

Where morainal débris covers thousands of acres, it is probable that valuable mineral veins were in some cases covered, prospecting prevented, and mineral wealth lost; but on the other hand, the erosion done by the glacier, often cutting down several hundred feet, has in many cases uncovered leads which otherwise probably would have been left buried beyond search. Then, too, millions of dollars of placer gold have been washed from moraines.

In addition to the work of making and giving

the mountains flowing lines of beauty, the glaciers added inconceivably to the richness of the earth's resources by creating vast estates of soil. It is probable that glaciers have supplied one half of the productive areas of the earth with soil; the mills of the glaciers have ground as much rock-flour — soil — for the earth as wind, frost, heat, and rain, — all the weathering forces. This flour and other coarser glacial grindings were quickly changed by the chemistry of Nature into plant-food, — the staff of life for forests and flowers.

Glaciers have not only ground the soil but in many places have carried this and spread it out hundreds of miles from the place where the original raw rocks were obtained. Wind and water have done an enormous amount of work sorting out the soil in moraines and, leaving the boulders behind, this soil was scattered and sifted far and wide to feed the hungry plant-life.

At last the Glacial Winter ended, and each year more snow melted and evaporated than fell. Snow-line retreated up the slopes and finally became broken, even in the heights. To-day, in the Rockies, there are only a dozen or so small glaciers, mere fragments of the once great ice cap which originally covered deeply all the higher places and slopes, and extended unbroken for hundreds of miles, pierced strangely with a few sharp peaks.

The small remaining glaciers in the Rocky Mountains lie in sheltered basins or cirques in the summits and mostly above the altitude of thirteen thousand feet. These are built and supplied by the winds which carry and sweep snow to them from off thousands of acres of treeless, barren summits. The present climate of these mountains is very different from what it was ages ago. Then for a time the annual snowfall was extremely heavy. Each year the sun and the wind removed only a part of the snow which fell during the year. This icy remainder was added to the left-over of preceding years until the accumulation was of vast depth and weight.

On the summit slopes this snow appears to have been from a few hundred to a few thousand feet deep. Softened from the saturation of melting and compressed from its own weight, it became a stratum of ice. This overlay the summit of the main ranges, and was pierced by only a few of the higher, sharper peaks which were sufficiently steep to be stripped of snow by snowslides and the wind.

The weight of this superimposed icy stratum was immense; it was greater than the bottom layers could support. Ice is plastic — rubbery — if sufficient pressure or weight be applied. Under the enormous pressure the bottom layers started to crawl or flow from beneath like squeezed dough. This forced mass moved outward and downward in the direction of the least resistance, — down the slope. Thus a glacier is conceived and born.

Numbers of these glaciers — immense serpents and tongues of ice — extended down the slopes, in places miles beyond the line of perpetual snow. Some of these were miles in length, a thousand or more feet wide, and hundreds of feet deep, and they forced and crushed their way irresistibly. It is probable they had a sustained, continuous flow for centuries.

A glacier is one of the natural wonders of the

world and well might every one pay a visit to one of these great earth-sculpturers. The time to visit a glacier is during late summer, when the snows of the preceding winter are most completely removed from the surface. With the snows removed, the beauty of the ice and its almost stratified make-up are revealed. The snow, too, conceals the yawning *bergschlunds* and the dangerous, splendid crevasses. A visit to one of these ponderous, patient, and effective monsters is not without danger; concealed crevasses, or thinly covered icy caverns, or recently deposited and insecurely placed boulders on the moraines are potent dangers that require vigilance to avoid. However, the careful explorer will find one of these places far safer than the city's chaotic and crowded street.

For the study of old glacier records few places can equal the Estes Park district in Colorado. The Arapahoe, on Arapahoe Peak, Colorado, is an excellent glacier to visit. It is characteristic and is easy of access. It is close to civilization, — within a few miles of a railroad, — is comprehensively situated, and is amid some of the grandest

A CREVASSE

scenery in the Rocky Mountains. It has been mapped and studied, and its rate of movement and many other things concerning it are accurately known. It is the abstract and brief chronicle of the Ice Age, a key to all the glacier ways and secrets.

In the Arapahoe Glacier one may see the cirque in which the snow is deposited or drifted by the wind; and the bergschlund-yawn — crack of separation — made by glacier ice where it moves away from the névé or snowy ice above. In walking over the ice in summer one may see or descend into the crevasses. These deep, wide cracks, miniature cañons, are caused by the ice flowing over inequalities in the surface. At the end of this glacier one may see the terminal moraine, — a raw, muddy pile of powdered, crushed, and rounded rocks. Farther along down the slope one may see the lakes that were made, the rocks that were polished, and the lateral moraine deposited by the glacier in its bigger days, — times when the Ice King almost conquered the earth.

In the Rocky Mountains the soil and morainal débris were transported only a few miles, while the Wisconsin and Iowa glaciers brought thousands of acres of rich surfacing, now on the productive farms of Ohio, Illinois, and Iowa, from places hundreds of miles to the north in Canada. In the Rocky Mountains most of the forests are growing in soil or moraines that were ground and distributed by glaciers. Thus the work of the glaciers has made the earth and the mountains far more useful in addition to giving them gentler influences, — charming lakes and flowing landscape lines. It is wonderful that the mighty worker and earth-shaper, the Ice King, should have used snowflakes for edge-tools, millstones, and crushing stamps!

To know the story of the Ice King — to be able to understand and restore the conditions that made lakes and headlands, moraines and fertile fields — will add mightily to the enjoyment of a visit to the Rocky Mountains, the Alps, the coasts and mountains of Norway and New England, Alaska's unrivaled glacier realm, or the extraordinary ice sculpturing in the Yosemite National Park.

The Maker of Scenery and Soil

Edward Orton, Jr., formerly State Geologist of Ohio, who spent weeks toiling over and mapping the Mills Moraine on the east slope of Long's Peak, gave a glimpse of what one may feel and enjoy from nature investigation in his closing remarks concerning this experience. He said, "If one adds to the physical pleasures of mountaineering, the intellectual delight of looking with the seeing eye, of explaining, interpreting, and understanding the gigantic forces which have wrought these wonders; if by these studies one's vision may be extended past the sublime beauties of the present down through the dim ages of the past until each carved and bastioned peak tells a romance above words; if by communion with this greatness, one's soul is uplifted and attuned into fuller accord with the great cosmic forces of which we are the higher manifestation, then mountaineering becomes not a pastime but an inspiration."

A Rainy Day at the Stream's Source

A Rainy Day at the Stream's Source

To spend a day in the rain at the source of a stream was an experience I had long desired, for the behavior of the waters in collecting and hurrying down slopes would doubtless show some of Nature's interesting ways. On the Rockies no spot seemed quite so promising as the watershed on which the St. Vrain made its start to the sea. This had steep and moderate slopes, rock ledges, and deep soil; and about one half of its five thousand acres was covered with primeval forest, while the remainder had been burned almost to barrenness by a fierce forest fire. Here were varied and contrasting conditions to give many moods to the waters, and all this display could easily be seen during one active day.

June was the month chosen, since in the region of the St. Vrain that is the rainiest part of the year. After thoroughly exploring the ground

The Spell of the Rockies

I concluded to go down the river a few miles and make headquarters in a new sawmill. There I spent delightful days in gathering information concerning tree-growth and in making biographical studies of several veteran logs, as the saw ripped open and revealed their life-scrolls.

One morning I was awakened by the pelting and thumping of large, widely scattered rain-drops on the roof of the mill. Tree stories were forgotten, and I rushed outdoors. The sky was filled with the structureless gloom of storm-cloud, and the heavy, calm air suggested rain. "We'll get a wetting such as you read of, to-day!" declared the sawmill foreman, as I made haste to start for the wilds.

I plunged into the woods and went eagerly up the dim, steep mountain trail which kept close company with the river St. Vrain. Any doubts concerning the strength of the storm were quickly washed away. My dry-weather clothes were swiftly soaked, but with notebook safe under my hat, I hastened to gain the "forks" as soon as possible, enjoying the general downpour and the softened noise that it made through the woods. I had often been out in rains on the Rockies, but this one was wetting the earth with less effort than any I had ever experienced. For half an hour no air stirred; then, while crossing a small irregular opening in the woods, I was caught in a storm-centre of wrangling winds and waters, and now and then their weight would almost knock me over, until, like a sapling, I bowed, streaming, in the storm. The air was full of "water-dust," and, once across the open, I made haste to hug a tree, hoping to find a breath of air that was not saturated to strangulation.

Neither bird nor beast had been seen, nor did I expect to come upon any, unless by chance my movements drove one from its refuge; but while I sat on a sodden log, reveling in elemental moods and sounds, a water-ouzel came flying along. He alighted on a boulder which the on-sweeping stream at my feet seemed determined to drown or dislodge, and, making his usual courtesies, he began to sing. His melody is penetrating; but so sustained was the combined

roar of the stream and the storm that there came
to me only a few notes of his energetic nesting-
time song. His expressive attitudes and gestures
were so harmoniously united with these, however, that I could not help feeling that he was
singing with all his might to the water, the woods,
and me.

Keeping close to the stream, I continued my
climb. My ear now caught the feeble note of a
robin, who was making discouraged and discon-
solate efforts at song, and it seemed to issue from
a throat clogged with wet cotton. Plainly the
world was not beautiful to him, and the attempt
at music was made to kill time or cheer himself
up.

The robin and the ouzel, — how I love them
both, and yet how utterly unlike they are! The
former usually chooses so poor a building-site,
anchors its nest so carelessly, or builds so clum-
sily, that the precious contents are often spilled
or the nest discovered by some enemy. His
mental make-up is such that he is prone to pre-
dict the worst possible outcome of any new
situation. The ouzel, on the other hand, is sweet

and serene. He builds his nest upon a rock and tucks it where search and sharp eyes may not find it. He appears indifferent to the comings and goings of beast or man, enjoys all weathers, seems entranced with life, and may sing every day of the year.

Up in the lower margin of the Engelmann spruce forest the wind now ceased and the clouds began to conserve their waters. The territory which I was about to explore is on the eastern summit slopes of the Rockies, between the altitudes of ninety-five hundred and twelve thousand feet. Most of these slopes were steep, and much of the soil had a basis of disintegrated granite. The forested and the treeless slopes had approximately equal areas, and were much alike in regard to soil, inclination, and altitude, while the verdure of both areas before the forest fire had been almost identical. The St. Vrain is formed by two branches flowing northeasterly and southeasterly, the former draining the treeless area and the latter the forested one. Below the junction, the united waters sweep away through the woods, but at it, and a short distance above, the fire had destroyed every living thing.

At the forks I found many things of interest. The branch with dark waters from the barren slopes was already swollen to many times its normal volume and was thick with sediment from the fire-scarred region. The stream with white waters from the forest had risen just a trifle, and there was only a slight stain visible. These noticeable changes were produced by an hour of rain. I dipped several canfuls from the deforested drainage fork, and after each had stood half a minute the water was poured off. The average quantity of sediment remaining was one fifth of a canful, while the white water from the forested slope deposited only a thin layer on the bottom of the can. It was evident that the forest was absorbing and delaying the water clinging to its soil and sediment. In fact, both streams carried so much suggestive and alluring news concerning storm effects on the slopes above that I determined to hasten on in order to climb over and watch them while they were dashed and drenched with rain.

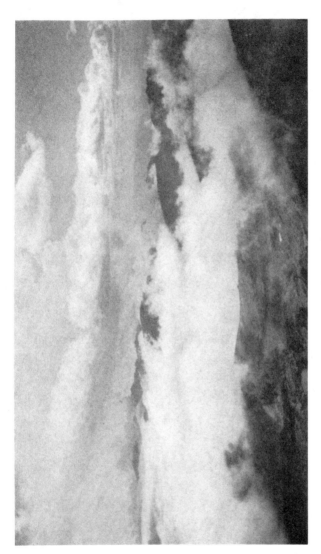

AMONG THE CLOUDS
Continental Divide, near Long's Peak

A Rainy Day

Planning to return and give more attention to the waters of both branches at this place, I started to inspect first the forested sides. The lower of these slopes were tilted with a twenty to twenty-five per cent grade, and covered with a primeval Engelmann spruce forest of tall, crowding trees, the age of which, as I had learned during previous visits, was only a few years less than two centuries.

The forest floor was covered with a thick carpet of litter, — one which the years had woven out of the wreckage of limbs and leaves. This, though loosely, coarsely woven, has a firm feeling when trodden during dry weather. To-day however, the forest floor seemed recently upholstered. It is absorbent; hence the water had filled the interstices and given elasticity. I cleared away some of this litter and found that it had an average depth of fifteen inches. The upper third lay loosely, but below it the weave was more compact and much finer than that on or near the surface. I judged that two inches of rain had fallen and had soaked to an average depth of eight inches. It was interesting to watch the water ooze from the broken walls of this litter, or humus, on the upper sides of the holes which I dug down into it. One of these was close to a bare, tilted slope of granite. As I stood watching the water slowly dripping from the broken humus and rapidly racing down the rocks, the thought came to me that, with the same difference in speed, the run-off from the deforested land might be breaking through the levees at New Orleans before the water from these woods escaped and got down as far as the sawmill.

The forest might well proclaim: "As long as I stand, my countless roots shall clutch and clasp the soil like eagles' claws and hold it on these slopes. I shall add to this soil by annually creating more. I shall heave it with my growing roots, loosen and cover it with litter rugs, and maintain a porous, sievelike surface that will catch the rain and so delay and distribute these waters that at the foot of my slope perennial springs will ever flow quietly toward the sea. Destroy me, and on stormy days the waters may wash away the unanchored soil as they run unresisted down the slopes, to form a black, destructive flood in the home-dotted valley below."

The summit of the forested slope was comparatively smooth where I gained it, and contained a few small, ragged-edged, grassy spaces among its spruces and firs. The wind was blowing and the low clouds pressed, hurried along the ground, whirled through the grassy places, and were driven and dragged swiftly among the trees. I was in the lower margin of cloud, and it was like a wet, gray night. Nothing could be seen clearly, even at a few feet, and every breath I took was like swallowing a saturated sponge.

These conditions did not last long, for a wind-surge completely rent the clouds and gave me a glimpse of the blue, sun-filled sky. I hurried along the ascending trend of the ridge, hoping to get above the clouds, but they kept rising, and after I had traveled half a mile or more I gave it up. Presently I was impressed with the height of an exceptionally tall spruce that stood in the centre of a group of its companions. At once I decided to climb it and have a look over the country and cloud from its swaying top.

When half way up, the swift manner in which the tree was tracing seismographic lines through the air awakened my interest in the trunk that was holding me. Was it sound or not? At the foot appearances gave it good standing. The exercising action of ordinary winds probably toughens the wood fibres of young trees, but this one was no longer young, and the wind was high. I held an ear against the trunk and heard a humming whisper which told only of soundness. A blow with broad side of my belt axe told me that it rang true and would stand the storm and myself.

The sound brought a spectator from a spruce with broken top that stood almost within touching distance of me. In this tree was a squirrel home, and my axe had brought the owner from his hole. What an angry, comic midget he was, this Frémont squirrel! With fierce whiskers and a rattling, choppy, jerky chatter, he came out on a dead limb that pointed toward me, and made a rush as though to annihilate me or to

cause me to take hurried flight; but as I held
on he found himself more "up in the air" than I
was. He stopped short, shut off his chatter, and
held himself at close range facing me, a picture
of furious study. This scene occurred in a brief
period that was undisturbed by either wind or
rain. We had a good look at each other. He was
every inch alive, but for a second or two both
his place and expression were fixed. He sat with
eyes full of telling wonder and with face that
showed intense curiosity. A dash of wind and
rain ended our interview, for after his explosive
introduction neither of us had uttered a sound.
He fled into his hole, and from this a moment
later thrust forth his head; but presently he
subsided and withdrew. As I began to climb
again, I heard muffled expletives from within his
tree that sounded plainly like "Fool, fool, fool!"

The wind had tried hard to dislodge me, but,
seated on the small limbs and astride the slender
top, I held on. The tree shook and danced;
splendidly we charged, circled, looped, and an-
gled; such wild, exhilarating joy I have not elsewhere experienced. At all times I could feel in

the trunk a subdued quiver or vibration, and I half believe that a tree's greatest joys are the dances it takes with the winds.

Conditions changed while I rocked there; the clouds rose, the wind calmed, and the rain ceased to fall. Thunder occasionally rumbled, but I was completely unprepared for the blinding flash and explosive crash of the bolt that came. The violent concussion, the wave of air which spread from it like an enormous, invisible breaker, almost knocked me over. A tall fir that stood within fifty feet of me was struck, the top whirled off, and the trunk split in rails to the ground. I quickly went back to earth, for I was eager to see the full effect of the lightning's stroke on that tall, slender evergreen cone. With one wild, mighty stroke, in a second or less, the century-old tree tower was wrecked.

Leaving this centenarian, I climbed up the incline a few hundred feet higher and started out through the woods to the deforested side. Though it was the last week in June, it was not long before I was hampered with snow. Ragged patches, about six feet deep, covered more than half of the forest floor. This was melting rapidly and was "rotten" from the rain, so that I quickly gave up the difficult task of fording it and made an abrupt descent until below the snow-line, where I again headed for the fire-cleared slopes.

As I was leaving the wood, the storm seemed to begin all over again. The rain at first fell steadily, but soon slackened, and the lower cloud-margins began to drift through the woods. Just before reaching the barrens I paused to breathe in a place where the trees were well spaced, and found myself facing a large one with deeply furrowed bark and limbs plentifully covered with short, fat, blunt needles. I was at first puzzled to know what kind it was, but at last I recognized it as a Douglas fir or "Oregon pine." I had never before seen this species at so great an altitude, — approximately ten thousand feet. It was a long distance from home, but it stood so contentedly in the quiet rain that I half expected to hear it remark, "The traditions of my family are mostly associated with gray, growing days of this kind."

The Spell of the Rockies

Out on the barren slopes the few widely scattered, fire-killed, fire-preserved trees with broken arms stood partly concealed and lonely in the mists. After zigzagging for a time over the ruins, I concluded to go at once to the uppermost side and thence down to the forks. But the rain was again falling, and the clouds were so low and heavy that the standing skeleton trees could not be seen unless one was within touching distance. There was no wind or lightning, only a warm, steady rain. It was, in fact, so comfortable that I sat down to enjoy it until a slackening should enable me better to see the things I most wanted to observe.

There was no snow about, and three weeks before at the same place I had found only one small drift which was shielded and half-covered with shelving rock. The dry Western air is insatiable and absorbs enormous quantities of water, and, as the Indians say, "eats snow." The snowless area about me was on a similar slope and at about the same altitude as the snow-filled woods, so the forest is evidently an effective check upon the ravenous winds.

A Rainy Day

Now the rain almost ceased, and I began to descend. The upper gentle slopes were completely covered with a filmy sheet of clear water which separated into tattered torrents and took on color. These united and grew in size as they progressed from the top, and each was separated from its companions by ridges that widened and gulches that deepened as down the sides they went. The waters carried most of the eroded material away, but here and there, where they crossed a comparatively level stretch, small deposits of gravel were made or sandbars and deltas formed.

Occasionally I saw miniature landslides, and, hoping for a larger one to move, I hurried downward. Knowing that the soil is often deep at the foot of crags on account of contributions from above, together with the protection from erosion which the cliffs gave, I endeavored to find such a place. While searching, I had occasion to jump from a lower ledge on a cliff to the deposit below. The distance to the slope and its real pitch were minimized by the mists. After shooting through the air for at least thrice the supposed distance to the slope, I struck heavily and loosened several rods of a landslide. I tumbled off the back of it, but not before its rock points had made some impressions.

I sought safety and a place of lookout on a crag, and picked bits of granite gravel from my anatomy. Presently I heard a muffled creaking, and looked up to see a gigantic landslide starting. At first it moved slowly, seemed to hesitate, then slid faster, with its stone-filled front edge here and there doubling and rolling under; finally the entire mass broke into yawning, ragged fissures as it shot forward and plunged over a cliff. Waiting until most of the straggling, detached riffraff had followed, I hastened to examine the place just evacuated. In getting down I disturbed a ground-hog from his rock point, and found that he was in the same attitude and position I had seen him holding just before the slide started, so that the exhibition had merely caused him to move his eyes a little.

In the cracks and crevices of the glaciated rock-slope from which this mass had slid, there were broken, half-decayed roots and numerous marks which showed where other roots had held. It seems probable that if the grove which sustained them had not been destroyed by fire, they in turn would have anchored and held securely the portion of land which had just slipped away.

I went over the lower slopes of the burned area and had a look at numerous new-made gullies, and near the forks I measured a large one. It was more than a hundred feet long, two to four feet wide, and, over the greater part of its length, more than four feet deep. It was eroded by the late downpour, and its misplaced material, after being deposited by the waters, would of itself almost call for an increase of the river and harbor appropriations.

Late in the afternoon, with the storm breaking, I stopped and watched the largest torrent from the devastated region pour over a cliff. This waterfall more nearly represented a liquefied landslide, for it was burdened with sediment and spoils. As it rushed wildly over, it carried enormous quantities of dirt, gravel, and other earthy wreckage, and some of the stones were as large as a man's hat. Now and then there was a slackening, but these momentary subsidences were followed by explosive out-pourings with which mingled large pieces of charred or half-decayed wood, sometimes closely pursued by a small boulder or some rock-fragments. Surely, these deforested slopes were heavy contributors to the millions of tons of undesirable matter that annually went in to fill the channel and vex the current of the Mississippi!

These demonstrations brought to mind a re-mark of an army engineer to the effect that the "Western forest fires had resulted in filling the Missouri River channel full of dissolved Rocky Mountains." The action of the water on this single burned area suggested that ten thousand other fireswept heights must be rapidly dimin-ishing. At all events, it is evident that, unless this erosion is stopped, boats before long will hardly find room to enter the Mississippi. It now became easier to account for the mud-filled channel of the great river, and also for the in-

numerable bars that display their broad backs
above its shallow, sluggish water. Every smooth
or fluted fill in this great stream tells of a ragged
gulch or a roughened, soilless place somewhere
on a slope at one of its sources.

What a mingling of matter makes up the mud
of the Mississippi, — a soil mixture from twenty
States, the blended richness of ten thousand
slopes! Coming up the "Father of Waters,"
and noting its obstructions of sediment and
sand, its embarrassment of misplaced material,
its dumps and deposits of soil, — monumental
ruins of wasted resources, — one may say,
"Here lies the lineal descendant of Pike's Peak;
here the greater part of an Ohio hill"; or, "A
flood took this from a terraced cotton-field, and
this from a farm in sunny Tennessee." A mud
flat itself might remark, "The thoughtless lum-
berman who caused my downfall is now in Congress urging river improvement"; and the shallow waters at the big bend could add, "Our
once deep channel was filled with soil from a
fire-scourged mountain. The minister whose
vacation fire caused this ruin is now a militant

missionary among the heathen of Cherry Blossom land."

Wondering if the ouzel's boulder had been rolled away, or if the deep hole above it, where the mill men caught trout, had been filled with wash, I decided to go at once and see, and then return for a final look about the forks. Yes, the boulder was missing, apparently buried, for the hole was earth-filled and the trout gone. So it was evident that forests were helpful even to the fish in the streams. I took off my hat to the trees and started back to the junction. On the way I resolved to tell the men in the mill that a tree is the most useful thing that grows, and that floods may be checked by forests.

The storm was over and the clouds were retreating. On a fallen log that lay across the main stream I lingered and watched the dark and white waters mingle. The white stream was slowly rising, while the dark one was rapidly falling. In a few days the one from the barren slopes would be hardly alive, while the other from among the trees would be singing a song full of strength as it swept on toward the sea.

FULL STREAMS

A Rainy Day

The forest-born stream is the useful and beautiful one. It has a steady flow of clear water, and fishermen cheerfully come to its green, mossy banks. The buildings along its course are safe from floods, and are steadily served with the power of its reliable flow; its channel is free from mud and full of water; it allows the busy boats of commerce freely to come and go; in countless ways it serves the activities of man. It never causes damage, and always enriches and gladdens the valley through which it flows on to the sea.

A song roused me from my revery. The sky was almost clear, and the long, ragged shadows of the nearest peaks streamed far toward the east. Not a breath of air stirred. Far away a hermit thrush was singing, while a thousand spruces stood and listened. In the midst of this a solitaire on the top of a pine tree burst out in marvelous melody.

The Fate of a Tree Seed

The Fate of a Tree Seed

THE ripened seeds of trees are sent forth with many strange devices and at random for the unoccupied and fertile places of the earth. There are six hundred kinds of trees in North America, and each of these equips its seeds in a peculiar way, that they may take advantage of wind, gravity, water, birds, or beasts to transport them on their home-seeking journey.

The whole seed-sowing story is a fascinating one. Blindly, often thick as snow, the seeds go forth to seek their fortune, — to find a rooting-place. All are in danger, many are limited as to time, and the majority are restricted to a single effort. A few, however, have a complex and novel equipment and with this make a long, romantic, and sometimes an adventurous journey, colonizing at last some strange land far from the place of their birth. Commonly, however, this journey is brief, and usually after one short fall or flight the seed comes to rest where it will sprout or perish. Generally it dies.

One autumn afternoon in southeastern Missouri, seated upon some driftwood on the shallow margin of the Mississippi, I discovered a primitive craft that was carrying a colony of adventurous tree seeds down the mighty river. As I watched and listened, the nuts pattered upon the fallen leaves and the Father of Waters purled and whispered as he slipped his broad yellow-gray current almost silently to the sea. Here and there a few broad-backed sandbars showed themselves above the surface, as though preparing to rise up and inquire what had become of the water.

This primitive craft was a log that drifted low and heavy, end on with the current. It was going somewhere with a small cargo of tree seeds. Upon a broken upraised limb of the log sat a kingfisher. As it drifted with the current, breezes upon the wooded hill-tops decorated the autumn air with deliberately falling leaves and floating winged seeds. The floating log pointed straight for a sand-bar upon which other logs and snags were stranded. I determined, when it should come aground, to see the character of the cargo that it carried.

Now and then, as I sat there, the heavy round nuts like merry boys came bounding and rattling down the hillside, which rose from the water's edge. Occasionally as a nut dropped from the tree-top he struck a limb spring board and from this made a long leap outward for a roll down the hillside. These nuts were walnut and hickory; and like most heavy nuts they traveled by rolling, floating, and squirrel carriage.

One nut dropped upon a low limb, glanced far outward, and landed upon a log, from which it bounced outward and went bouncing down the hillside *aplunk* into the river. Slowly it rolled this way and that in the almost currentless water. At last it made up its mind, and, with the almost invisible swells, commenced to float slowly toward the floating log out in the river. By and by the current caught it, carried it toward and round the sand-bar, to float away with the onsweep toward the sea. This nut may have been carried a few miles or a few hundred before it went ashore on the bank of the river or landed upon some romantic island to sprout and grow. Seeds often are carried by rivers and then successfully planted, after many stops and advances, far from the parent tree.

The log hesitated as it approached the sandbar, as if cautiously smelling with its big, rooty nose; but at last it swung round broadside, and sleepily allowed the current to put it to bed upon the sand. As a tree, this log had lived on the banks of the Mississippi or one of its tributaries, in Minnesota. While standing it had for a time served as a woodpecker home. In one of the larger excavations made by these birds, I found some white pine cones and other seeds from the north that had been stored by bird or squirrel. A long voyage these seeds had taken; they may have continued the journey, landing at last to grow in sunny Tennessee; or they may have sunk to the bottom of the river or even have perished in the salt waters of the Gulf.

In climbing up the steep hillside above the river, I found many nests of hickory and walnuts against the upper side of fallen logs. Upon the

The Fate of a Tree Seed

level hill-top the ground beneath the tree was thickly covered with fallen nuts; only a few of these had got a tree's length away from the parent. Occasionally, however, a wind-gust used a long, slender limb as a sling, and flung the attached nuts afar.

The squirrels were active, laying up a hoard of nuts for winter. Many a walnut, hickory, or butternut tree at some distant place may have grown from an uneaten or forgotten nut which the squirrels carried away.

The winged seeds are the ones that are most widely scattered. These are grown by many kinds of trees. From May until midwinter trees of this kind are giving their little atoms of life to the great seed-sower, the wind. Most winged seeds have one wing for each seed and commonly each makes but one flight. Generally the lighter the seed and the higher the wind, the farther the seed will fly or be blown.

In May the silver maple starts the flight of winged seeds. This tree has a seed about the size of a peanut, provided with a one-sided wing as large as one's thumb. It sails away from the tree, settling rapidly toward the earth with heavy end downward, whirling round and round as it falls. Red maple seeds ripen in June, but not until autumn does the hard maple send its winged ones forth from amid the painted leaves.

The seed of an ash tree is like a dart. In the different ashes these are of different lengths, but all have two-edged wings which in calm weather dart the seed to the snowy earth; but in a lively wind they are tumbled and whirled about while being unceremoniously carried afar; this they do not mind, for at the first lull they right themselves and drop in good form to the earth.

Cottonwoods and willows send forth their seeds inclosed in a dainty puff or ball of silky cotton that is so light that the wind often carries it long distances. With the willow this device is so airy and dainty that it is easily entangled on twigs or grass and may never reach the earth. The willow seed, too, is so feeble that it will often perish inside twenty-four hours if it does not find a most favorable germinating-place. This makes but little difference to the willows, for they do not depend upon seeds for extension but upon the breaking off of roots or twigs by various agencies; these pieces of roots or twigs often are carried miles by streams, and take root perhaps at the first place where they go around.

The seeds of the sycamore are in balls attached to the limbs by a slender twiglet. The winter winds beat and thump these balls against the limbs, thus causing the seeds to loosen and to drop a few at a time to the earth. Each seed is a light little pencil which at one end is equipped with a whorl of hairs, — a parachute which delays its fall and thus enables the wind to carry it away from the parent tree.

The conifers — the pines, firs, and spruces — have ingeniously devised and developed their winged seeds for wind distribution. Most of these seeds are light, and each is attached to a dainty feather or wing which is used on its commencement day. These wings are as handsome as insects' wings, dainty enough for fairies; they are purple, plain brown, and spotted, and so balanced that they revolve or whirl, glinting in the autumn sun as they go on their adventurous wind-blown flight to the earth. A high wind may carry them miles.

With the pines and spruces the cones open one or a few scales at a time, so that the seeds from each cone are distributed through many days. The firs, however, carry cones that when ripe often collapse in the wind. The entire filling of seeds are thus dropped at once and fill the air with flocks of merry, diving, glinting wings. A heavy seed-crop in a coniferous forest gives a touch of poetry to the viewless air.

The lodge-pole pine is one of the most patient and philosophical seed-sowers in the forest. It is a prolific seed-producer and has a remarkable hoarding characteristic, — that of keeping its cones closed and holding on to them for years. Commonly a forest fire kills trees without consuming them. With the lodge-pole the fire frequently burns off the needles, leaving the tree standing, but it melts the sealing-wax on the cones. Thus the fire releases these seeds and they fall upon a freshly fire-cleaned soil, — a condition for them most favorable.

Although the cherry is without wings or a

The Fate of a Tree Seed

flying-machine of its own, it is rich enough to employ the rarest transportation in the world. With attractively colored and luscious pulp it hires many beautiful birds to carry it to new scenes. On the wings of the mockingbird and the hermit thrush, — what a happy and romantic way in which to seek the promised land!

Many kinds of pulp-covered seeds that are attractive and delicious when ripe are unpleasant to the taste while green; this protective measure guards them against being sown before they are ready or ripe. The instant persimmons are ripe, the trees are full of opossums which disseminate the ready-to-grow seeds; but Mr. 'Possum avoids the green and puckery persimmons!

The big tree is one of the most fruitful of seed-bearers. In a single year one of these may produce some millions of fertile seeds. These mature in comparatively small cones and, each seed being light as air, they are sometimes carried by high winds across ridges and ravines before being dropped to the earth.

The honey locust uses a peculiar device to

The Spell of the Rockies

secure wind assistance in pushing afar its long,
purplish pods with their heavy beanlike seeds.
This pod is not only flattened but crooked and
slightly twisted. Dropping from the tree in
midwinter, it often lands upon crusted snow.
Here on windy days it becomes a kind of crude
ice-boat and goes skimming along before the
wind; with its flattened, twisted surface it ever
presents a boosting-surface to the breeze.

The ironwood tree launches its seeds each
seated in the prow of a tiny boat, which floats
or careers away upon the invisible ocean of air,
sinking, after a rudderless voyage, to the earth.
The attachment to some seeds is bladder- or
balloon-like; tied helplessly to this, the seed is
cast forth briefly to wander with the wandering
winds.

The linden, or basswood, tree uses a mono-
plane for buoyancy. The basswood attaches or
suspends a number of seeds by slender threads
to the centre of a leaf; in autumn when this
falls it resists gravity for a time and ofttimes
with its clinging cargo alights far from the tree
which sent it forth.

The Fate of a Tree Seed

Burr- or hook-covered seeds may become attached to the backs of animals and thus be transported afar. One day in Colorado I disturbed a black bear in some willows more than a mile from the woods; as he ran over a grassy ridge three or four pine cones that had been hooked and entangled in his hair went spinning off. Seeds sometimes are internationally distributed by becoming attached by some sticky substance — pitch or dried mud — to the legs or feathers of birds. Cottonwood seed often has a long ride, though generally a fruitless one, by alighting in the hair of some animal. Sometimes a cone or nut becomes wedged between the hoofs of an animal and is carried about for days; taken miles before it is dropped, it grows a lone tree far from the nearest grove.

Though the witch-hazel is no longer invested with eerie charms, it still has its own peculiar way of doing things. It chooses to bloom alone in the autumn, just at the time its seeds are ripe and scattering. Assisted by the frost and the sun, it scatters its shotlike seeds with a series of snappy little explosions which fling them twelve to twenty feet from the capsule in which they ripen.

The mangrove trees of Florida germinate their seeds upon the tree and then drop little plants off into the water; here winds and currents may move them hither and yon as they blindly explore for a rooting-place.

The cocoanut tree covers its nuts with a kind of "excelsior" which prevents their breaking upon the rocks. This also facilitates the floating and transportation of the nut in the sea. When the breakers have flung it upon rocks or broken reefs, here its fibrous covering helps it cling until the young roots grow and anchor it securely.

Thus endlessly during all the seasons of the year the trees are sowing their ripened seed and sending them forth, variously equipped, blindly to seek a place in which they may live, perpetuate the species, and extend the forest.

It is well that nature sows seeds like a spendthrift. So many are the chances against the seed, so numerous are the destroying agencies, so few are the places in reach that are unoccupied, that perhaps not more than one seed in a million ever germinates, and hardly one tree in a thousand that starts to grow ever attains maturity. Through sheer force of numbers and continuous seed-scattering, the necessarily random methods of nature produce results; and where opportunity opens, trees promptly extend their holdings or reclaim a territory from which they have been driven.

Many times I have wandered through the coniferous forests in the mountains when the seeds were ripe and fluttering thick as snowflakes to the earth. Visiting ridges, slopes, and cañons, I have watched the pines, firs, and spruces closing a year's busy, invisible activity by merrily strewing the air and the earth with their fruits, — seeding for the centuries to come. One breathless autumn day I looked up into the blue sky from the bottom of a cañon. The golden air was as thickly filled with winged seeds as a perfect night with stars. A light local air-current made a milky way across this sky. Myriads of becalmed and suspended seeds were fixed stars. Some of the seeds, each with a filmy wing, hurried through elliptical orbits like comets as they settled to the earth; while innumerable others, as they came rotating down, were revolving through planetary orbits in this seed-sown field of space. Now and then a number of cones on a fir tree collapsed and precipitated into space a meteoric shower of slow-descending seeds and a hurried zigzag fall of heavier scales. Occasionally on a ridge-top a few of the lighter seeds would come floating upward through an air-chimney as though carried in an invisible smoke-column.

One windy day I crossed the mountains when a gale was driving millions of low-flying seeds before it. Away they swept down the slope, to whirl widely and flutter over the gulch where the wind-current dashed against the uprising mountain beyond. Most of the seeds were flung to the earth along the way or dropped in the bottom of the gulch; a few, however, were carried by the swift uprushing current up and across the mountain and at last scattered on the opposite side.

When the last seed of the year has fallen, how thickly the woodland regions are sown broad-

The Fate of a Tree Seed

cast with seeds! Only a few of these will have landed in a hospitable place. The overwhelmingly majority fell in the water to drown or on rock ledges or other places to starve or wither. The few fortunate enough to find unoccupied and fertile places will still have to reckon with devouring insects and animals. How different may be the environment of two seedlings sprung from seeds grown on the selfsame tree! On their commencement day two little atoms of life may be separated by the wind: one finds shelter and fertile earth; the other roots in a barely livable place on the cold, stormbeaten heights of timber-line. Both use their inherent energy and effort to the utmost. One becomes a forest monarch; the other a dwarf, uncouth and ugly.

In a Mountain Blizzard

In a Mountain Blizzard

At the close of one of our winter trips, my collie Scotch and I started across the continental divide of the Rocky Mountains in face of weather conditions that indicated a snow-storm or a blizzard before we could gain the other side. We had eaten the last of our food twenty-four hours before and could no longer wait for fair weather. So off we started to scale the snowy steeps of the cold, gray heights a thousand feet above. The mountains already were deeply snow-covered and it would have been a hard trip even without the discomforts and dangers of a storm.

I was on snowshoes and for a week we had been camping and tramping through the snowy forests and glacier meadows at the source of Grand River, two miles above the sea. The primeval Rocky Mountain forests are just as near to Nature's heart in winter as in summer. I had found so much to study and enjoy that the long distance from a food-supply, even when the last mouthful was eaten, had not aroused me to the seriousness of the situation. Scotch had not complained, and appeared to have the keenest collie interest in the tracks and trails, the scenes and silences away from the haunts of man. The snow lay seven feet deep, but by keeping in my snowshoe tracks Scotch easily followed me about. Our last camp was in the depths of an alpine forest at an altitude of ten thousand feet. Here, though zero weather prevailed, we were easily comfortable beside a fire under the protection of an overhanging cliff.

After a walk through woods the sun came blazing in our faces past the snow-piled crags on Long's Peak, and threw slender blue shadows of the spiry spruces far out in a white glacier meadow to meet us. Rëentering the tall but open woods, we saw, down the long aisles and limb-arched avenues, a forest of tree columns, entangled in sunlight and shadow, standing on a snowy marble floor.

We were on the Pacific slope, and our plan was to cross the summit by the shortest way between

ON GRAND RIVER, MIDDLE PARK, IN WINTER

In a Mountain Blizzard

timber-line and timber-line on the Atlantic side. This meant ascending a thousand feet, descending an equal distance, traveling five miles amid bleak, rugged environment. Along the treeless, gradual ascent we started, realizing that the last steep icy climb would be dangerous and defiant. Most of the snow had slid from the steeper places, and much of the remainder had blown away. Over the unsheltered whole the wind was howling. For a time the sun shone dimly through the wind-driven snow-dust that rolled from the top of the range, but it disappeared early behind wild, windswept clouds.

After gaining a thousand feet of altitude through the friendly forest, we climbed out and up above the trees on a steep slope at timber-line. This place, the farthest up for trees, was a picturesque, desolate place. The dwarfed, gnarled, storm-shaped trees amid enormous snow-drifts told of endless, and at times deadly, struggles of the trees with the elements. Most of the trees were buried, but here and there a leaning or a storm-distorted one bent bravely above the snows.

The Spell of the Rockies

At last we were safely on a ridge and started merrily off, hoping to cover speedily the three miles of comparatively level plateau.

How the wind did blow! Up more than eleven thousand feet above the sea, with not a tree to steady or break, it had a royal sweep. The wind appeared to be putting forth its wildest efforts to blow us off the ridge. There being a broad way, I kept well from the edges. The wind came with a dash and heavy rush, first from one quarter, then from another. I was watchful and faced each rush firmly braced. Generally, this preparedness saved me; but several times the wind apparently expanded or exploded beneath me, and, with an upward toss, I was flung among the icy rocks and crusted snows. Finally I took to dropping and lying flat whenever a violent gust came ripping among the crags.

There was an arctic barrenness to this alpine ridge, — not a house within miles, no trail, and here no tree could live to soften the sternness of the landscape or to cheer the traveler. The way was amid snowy piles, icy spaces, and wind-swept crags.

In a Mountain Blizzard

The wind slackened and snow began to fall just as we were leaving the smooth plateau for the broken part of the divide. The next mile of way was badly cut to pieces with deep gorges from both sides of the ridge. The inner ends of several of these broke through the centre of the ridge and extended beyond the ends of the gorges from the opposite side. This made the course a series of sharp, short zigzags.

We went forward in the flying snow. I could scarcely see, but felt that I could keep the way on the broken ridge between the numerous rents and cañons. On snowy, icy ledges the wind took reckless liberties. I wanted to stop but dared not, for the cold was intense enough to freeze one in a few minutes.

Fearing that a snow-whirl might separate us, I fastened one end of my light, strong rope to Scotch's collar and the other end to my belt. This proved to be fortunate for both, for while we were crossing an icy, though moderate, slope, a gust of wind swept me off my feet and started us sliding. It was not steep, but was so slippery I could not stop, nor see where the slope ended,

313

and I grabbed in vain at the few icy projections. Scotch also lost his footing and was sliding and rolling about, and the wind was hurrying us along, when I threw myself flat and dug at the ice with fingers and toes. In the midst of my unsuccessful efforts we were brought to a sudden stop by the rope between us catching over a small rock-point that was thrust up through the ice. Around this in every direction was smooth, sloping ice; this, with the high wind, made me wonder for a moment how we were to get safely off the slope. The belt axe proved the means, for with it I reached out as far as I could and chopped a hole in the ice, while with the other hand I clung to the rock-point. Then, returning the axe to my belt, I caught hold in the chopped place and pulled myself forward, repeating this until on safe footing.

In oncoming darkness and whirling snow I had safely rounded the ends of two gorges and was hurrying forward over a comparatively level stretch, with the wind at my back boosting along. Scotch was running by my side and evidently was trusting me to guard against all

In a Mountain Blizzard

dangers. This I tried to do. Suddenly, however, there came a fierce dash of wind and whirl of snow that hid everything. Instantly I flung myself flat, trying to stop quickly. Just as I did this I caught the strange, weird sound made by high wind as it sweeps across a cañon, and at once realized that we were close to a storm-hidden gorge. I stopped against a rock, while Scotch slid in and was hauled back with the rope.

The gorge had been encountered between two out-thrusting side gorges, and between these in the darkness I had a cold time feeling my way out. At last I came to a cairn of stones which I recognized. The way had been missed by only a few yards, but this miss had been nearly fatal.

Not daring to hurry in the darkness in order to get warm, I was becoming colder every moment. I still had a stiff climb between me and the summit, with timber-line three rough miles beyond. To attempt to make it would probably result in freezing or tumbling into a gorge. At last I realized that I must stop and spend the night in a snow-drift. Quickly kicking and trampling a trench in a loose drift, I placed my elk-skin sleeping-bag therein, thrust Scotch into the bag, and then squeezed into it myself.

I was almost congealed with cold. My first thought after warming up was to wonder why I had not earlier remembered the bag. Two in a bag would guarantee warmth, and with warmth a snow-drift on the crest of the continent would not be a bad place in which to lodge for the night.

The sounds of wind and snow beating upon the bag grew fainter and fainter as we were drifted and piled over with the latter. At the same time our temperature rose, and before long it was necessary to open the flap of the bag slightly for ventilation.

At last the sounds of the storm could barely be heard. Was the storm quieting down, or was its roar muffled and lost in the deepening cover of snow, was the unimportant question occupying my thoughts when I fell asleep.

Scotch awakened me in trying to get out of the bag. It was morning. Out we crawled, and,

In a Mountain Blizzard

standing with only my head above the drift, I found the air still and saw a snowy mountain world all serene in the morning sun. I hastily adjusted sleeping-bag and snowshoes, and we set off for the final climb to the summit.

The final one hundred feet or so rose steep, jagged, and ice-covered before me. There was nothing to lay hold of; every point of vantage was plated and coated with non-prehensible ice. There appeared only one way to surmount this icy barrier and that was to chop toe and hand holes from the bottom to the top of this icy wall, which in places was close to vertical. Such a climb would not be especially difficult or dangerous for me, but could Scotch do it? He could hardly know how to place his feet in the holes or on the steps properly; nor could he realize that a slip or a misstep would mean a slide and a roll to death.

Leaving sleeping-bag and snowshoes with Scotch, I grasped my axe and chopped my way to the top and then went down and carried bag and snowshoes up. Returning for Scotch, I started him climbing just ahead of me, so that I

317

could boost and encourage him. We had gained only a few feet when it became plain that sooner or later he would slip and bring disaster to both. We stopped and descended to the bottom for a new start.

Though the wind was again blowing a gale, I determined to carry him. His weight was forty pounds, and he would make a top-heavy load and give the wind a good chance to upset my balance and tip me off the wall. But, as there appeared no other way, I threw him over my shoulder and started up.

Many times Scotch and I had been in ticklish places together, and more than once I had pulled him up rocky cliffs on which he could not find footing. Several times I had carried him over gulches on fallen logs that were too slippery for him. He was so trusting and so trained that he relaxed and never moved while in my arms or on my shoulder.

Arriving at the place least steep, I stopped to transfer Scotch from one shoulder to the other. The wind was at its worst; its direction frequently changed and it alternately calmed and

SNOW AND SHADOW

then came on like an explosion. For several seconds it had been roaring down the slope; bracing myself to withstand its force from this direction, I was about moving Scotch, when it suddenly shifted to one side and came with the force of a breaker. It threw me off my balance and tumbled me heavily against the icy slope.

Though my head struck solidly, Scotch came down beneath me and took most of the shock. Instantly we glanced off and began to slide swiftly. Fortunately I managed to get two fingers into one of the chopped holes and held fast. I clung to Scotch with one arm; we came to a stop, both saved. Scotch gave a yelp of pain when he fell beneath me, but he did not move. Had he made a jump or attempted to help himself, it is likely that both of us would have gone to the bottom of the slope.

Gripping Scotch with one hand and clinging to the icy hold with the other, I shuffled about until I got my feet into two holes in the icy wall. Standing in these and leaning against the ice, with the wind butting and dashing, I attempted the ticklish task of lifting Scotch again to my

The Spell of the Rockies

shoulder — and succeeded. A minute later we paused to breathe on the summit's icy ridge, between two oceans and amid seas of snowy peaks.

A Midget in Fur

A Midget in Fur

THE Frémont squirrel is the most audacious and wide-awake of wild folk among whom I have lived. He appears to be ever up and doing, is intensely in earnest at all times and strongly inclined to take a serious view of things. Both the looks and manners of Mr. Frémont, *Sciurus fremonti*, proclaim for him a close relationship with the Douglas squirrel of California and the Pacific coast, the squirrel immortalized by John Muir.

His most popular name is "Pine Squirrel," and he is found through the pine and spruce forests of the Rocky Mountains and its spur ranges, between the foothills and timber-line; a vertical, or altitudinal, range of more than a mile. He assumes and asserts ownership of the region occupied. If you invade his forests he will see you first and watch you closely. Often he does this with simple curiosity, but more often he is irritated by your presence and issues a chattering protest while you are still at long range. If you continue to approach after this proclamation, he may come down on a low limb near by and give you as torrential and as abusive a "cussing" as trespasser ever received from irate owner.

Yet he is most ridiculously small to do all that he threatens to do. Of course he brags and bluffs, but these become admirable qualities in this little fellow who will ably, desperately defend his domain against heavy odds of size or numbers. Among the squirrels of the world he is one of the smallest. He is clad in gray and his coat perceptibly darkens in winter. His plumy tail, with a fringe of white hairs, is as airy as thistledown. He always appears clean and well-groomed.

Though in many ways a grizzly in miniature and apparently as untamable as a tiger, the Frémont quickly responds to kind advances. Near my cabin a number became so tame that they took peanuts from my hand, sometimes even following me to the cabin door for this purpose.

These squirrels occasionally eat mushrooms,

berries, and the inner bark of pine twigs, but they depend almost entirely upon conifer nuts or seeds, the greater part of these coming from the cones of pines and spruces. They start harvesting the cones in early autumn, so as to harvest all needed food for winter before the dry, ripened cones open and empty their tiny seeds. Deftly they dart through the tree-tops almost as swiftly as a hummingbird and as utterly indifferent to the dangers of falling. With polished blades of ivory they clip off the clinging, fruited cones. Happy, hopeful, harvest-home sounds the cones make as they drop and bounce on the dry floor of the autumn woods. Often a pair work together, one reaping the cones with his ivory cutters and the other carrying them home, each being a sheaf of grain of Nature's bundling.

When harvesting alone, Mr. Frémont is often annoyed by the chipmunks. These little rascals will persist in stealing the fallen cones, despite glaring eyes, irate looks, and deadly threats from the angry harvester above. When finally he comes tearing down to carry his terrible ultimatums into effect, the frightened chipmunks make haste to be off, but usually some one is overtaken and knocked sprawling with an accompanying rapid fire of denunciation.

One day I watched a single harvester who was busily, happily working. He cut off a number of cones before descending to gather them. These scattered widely like children playing hide-and-seek. One hid behind a log; another bounced into some brush and stuck two feet above the ground, while two others scampered far from the tree. The squirrel went to each in turn without the least hesitation or search and as though he had been to each spot a dozen times before.

A squirrel often displays oddities both in the place selected for storing the cones and the manner of their arrangement. Usually the cones are wisely hoarded both for curing and for preservation, by being stored a few in a place. This may be beneath a living tree or in an open space, placed one layer deep in the loose forest litter scarcely below the general level of the surface. They are also stowed both in and upon old logs and stumps. Sometimes they are placed in little nests with a half-dozen or so cones each; often

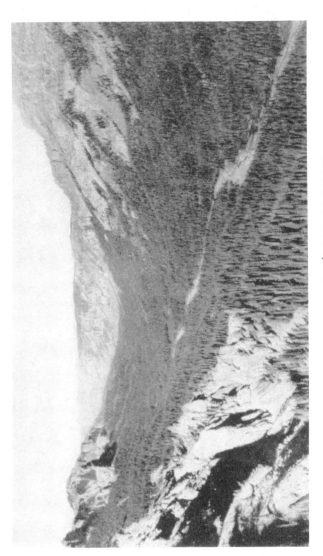

THE HOME OF THE FRÉMONT SQUIRREL

On the Little Cimarron

there are a dozen of these in a square yard. This scattering of the sap-filled cones, together with the bringing of each into contact with dry foreign substances, secures ventilation and assists the sappy cones to dry and cure; if closely piled, many of these moist cones would be lost through mould and decay.

The numbers of cones hoarded for winter by each squirrel varies with different winters and also with individuals. I have many times counted upwards of two hundred per squirrel. During years of scanty cone-crop the squirrels claim the entire crop. The outcry raised against the squirrel for preventing far extension, by consuming all the seeds, is I think in the same class as the cry against the woodpecker; it appears a cry raised by those who see only the harm without the accompanying good. The fact is that many of the cones are never eaten; more are stored than are wanted; some are forgotten, while others are left by the death of the squirrel. Thus many are stored and left uneaten in places where they are likely to germinate and produce trees. John Muir too believes that the Douglas and Frémont squirrels are beneficial to forest-extension.

Commonly the cones are stored in the same place year after year. In dining, also, the squirrel uses a log, limb, or stump year after year. Thus bushels of the slowly decaying scales and cobs accumulate in one place. It is not uncommon for these accumulations to cover a square rod to the depth of two feet.

I know of a few instances in which squirrels stowed cones in the edge of a brook beneath the water. One of these places being near my cabin, I kept track of it until the cones were used, which was in the spring. In early autumn the cones were frozen in, and there they remained, unvisited I think, until the break-up of the ice in April. Then a squirrel appeared, to drag them from their cold storage. He carried each by to his regular dining-place. Clasping the cone vertically, base up, in his fore paws, he snipped off the scales and ate the seeds beneath in regular order, turning the cone as he proceeded as though it were an ear of corn and he were eating the kernels.

A Midget in Fur

I have often waited to see a squirrel go for something to eat after a snowstorm. This he did in a matter-of-fact way. Without hunting or hesitation he went hopping across the snow to a spot immediately above his supplies, where he at once pawed his way down into the snow and came up with a cone.

In rambling the woods I have often heard these squirrels barking and "chickareeing" with wild hilarity, apparently from the pure joy of living. Then again they proclaimed my distant approach, or presence, with unnecessary vigor. The energetic protest they make against the trespasser in their woods, is often, if not always, taken by big game as a warning. Generally on hearing this the game will be all alert for some seconds, and occasionally will move off to a more commanding position. Sometimes birds will stop and listen when this tree-top sentinel shouts warnings which have often saved big game from being shot. Most hunters hate this squirrel.

There are brief periods in winter when these squirrels disappear for days at a time. The kind of weather does not appear to be a determining factor in this. During this disappearance they probably take a hibernating sleep; anyway, I have in a few cases seen them so soundly asleep that the fall and fracture of their tree did not awaken them. They sometimes live, temporarily at least, in holes in the ground, but the home is usually in a hollow limb or a cavern in a tree-trunk well toward the top of the tree. Commonly four young ones are brought forth at a birth. Cunning, happy midgets they are when first beginning their acquaintance with the wooded world, and taking sun baths on a high limb of their house tree.

Just how long they live no one appears to know. As pets they have been kept for ten years. A pair lived near my cabin for eight years, then disappeared. Whether they migrated or met a violent death, I never knew. There was another pair in the grove that I kept track of through eleven years. This grove was a wedge-shaped one of about ten acres that stood between two brooks. With but few exceptions, the trees were lodge-pole pine. My acquaintance with the pair began one day in early autumn. Both set up such a wild chatter as I approached the grove that I first thought that something was attacking them. Seated upon a log close to the tree which they occupied, I watched them for three or four hours. They in turn watched me. Failing to dislodge me by vehement denunciation, they quieted down and eyed me with intense curiosity. I sat perfectly still. Evidently they were greatly puzzled and unable to make out what I was and what of all things on earth it could be that I wanted. With beady eyes they stared at me from a number of positions in several trees. Occasionally in the midst of this silent, eager eying one would break out in a half-repressed and drawling bark that was unconsciously, nervously repeated at brief intervals.

The next day they silently allowed me to take a seat. After a brief stare they grew bold with curiosity and descended to the earth for a closer investigation. Pausing for a sharp look, both suddenly exploded with wild chatter and fled with a retchy barking to the tree-tops. In less than a month they took peanuts from my fingers. They were easily terrified by a loud noise or sudden movement. One day an acquaintance came to see me while I was in the grove with the squirrels. By way of heralding his approach, he flung a club which fell with a crash upon a brush pile alongside these most nervous fellows. They fled in terror, and it was two or three days before they would come near me again.

One year the grove cone-crop was a total failure. As a result, Mr. and Mrs. Frémont temporarily abandoned their old home and moved to new quarters on a mountainside about half a mile distant. The day they moved I was by the brook, watching a water-ouzel, when they chanced to cross on a fallen log near-by. In passing, one paused to give a hasty, half-glad, half-frightened, chattery bark of recognition. They hastened across the grassy open beyond as though they felt themselves in danger when out of the woods.

They made a home in an old snag, using places that were, I think, formerly used by woodpeckers. The afternoon of their arrival they commenced to harvest cones, which were abundant on the spruce trees around them. I often wondered if they made a preliminary trip and located a food-supply before moving, or if they simply started forth and stopped at the first favorable place.

The following summer they returned to their old quarters in the grove. The first time that I saw them they were sitting upon a log daintily making a breakfast of fresh mushrooms. They often ate the inner bark of pine twigs, and once I saw one of them eating wild raspberries. I never saw these, or any Frémont squirrel, robbing or trying to rob a bird's nest, and as I have never noticed a bird disturbed by their presence, I believe they are not guilty of this serious offense, as are most kinds of squirrels.

Through eleven years I occasionally fed them. Apparently full-grown at the time of our first meeting, they were active and agile to the last. After eleven years they showed but few and minor signs of aging.

One was shot by a gun-carrying visitor. While I was dismissing the gunner, my attention was attracted by the wailing of her mate when he found her lifeless body. His grief was most pitiful; among wild birds and animals I have never seen anything so pathetic. Almost humanly he stared at his mate; he fondled her and tried to coax her back to life, at times almost pleading and wailing. When I carried her off for burial he sat moveless and dazed. The following day I searched the grove, whistling and calling, but I never saw him again.

The Estes Park Region

The Estes Park Region

THE Estes Park region became famous for its scenery during the height of the Rocky Mountain gold-fever half a century ago. While Colorado was still a Territory, its scenes were visited by Helen Hunt, Anna Dickinson, and Isabella Bird, all of whom sang the praises of this great hanging wild garden.

The park is a natural one,—a mingling of meadows, headlands, groves, winding streams deeply set in high mountains whose forested steeps and snowy, broken tops stand high and bold above its romantic loveliness. It is a marvelous grouping of gentleness and grandeur; an eloquent, wordless hymn, that is sung in silent, poetic pictures; a sublime garden miles in extent and all arranged with infinite care.

Grace Greenwood once declared that the sky-line of this region, when seen from out in the Great Plains, loomed up like the Alps from the plains of Lombardy.

The Spell of the Rockies

Long's Peak, "King of the Rocky Mountains," dominates these scenes. Around this peak, within a radius of fifteen miles, is a striking and composite grouping of the best features of the Rocky Mountain scenery. Again and again I have explored every nook and height of this scenic mountain wilderness, enjoying its forests, lakes, and cañons during every month of the year.

Frost and fire have had much to do with its lines and landscapes. Ice has wrought bold sculptures, while fire made the graceful open gardens, forest-framed and flower-filled in the sun. The region was occupied by the Ice King during the last glacial period. Many rounded peaks, U-shaped, polished gorges, enormous morainal embankments, upwards of fifty lakes and tarns — almost the entire present striking landscape — were shaped through the ages by the slow sculpturing of the ice. Forest fires have made marked changes, and many of the wide poetic places — the grassy parks — in the woods are largely due to severe and repeated burnings.

LONG'S PEAK AND ESTES PARK

The Estes Park Region

This locality has been swept by fire again and again. Most of the forest is less than two hundred years of age. During the past two hundred years, beginning with 1707, there have been no less than seven forest fires, two of which appear to have swept over most of the region. There probably were other fires, the records of which have vanished. The dates of these scourges and in many cases the extent of their ravages were burned into the annual rings of a number of trees which escaped with their lives and lived on, carrying these fire-records down to us. These fires, together with the erosion which followed, had something to do with the topography and the scenery of this section. There are a few ugly scars from recent fires, but most of the burned areas were reforested with reasonable promptness. Some crags, however, may have lost for centuries their trees and vegetation. Other areas, though losing trees, gained in meadows. I am strongly inclined to ascribe much of the openness — the existence even — of Estes, Allen's, and Middle Parks to repeated fires, some of which probably were severe. Thus we may look down from the heights and enjoy the mingling beauty and grandeur of forest and meadow and still realize that fire, with all its destructiveness, may help to make the gardens of the earth.

A dozen species of trees form the forests of this section. These forests, delightfully inviting, cover the mountains below the altitude of eleven thousand feet. This rich robe, draping from the shoulders to the feet of the mountains, appears a dark purple from a distance. A great robe it hangs over every steep and slope, smooth, wrinkled, and torn; pierced with pinnacles and spires, gathered on terraces and headlands, uplifted on the swells, and torn by cañons. Here and there this forest is beautified with a ragged-edged grass-plot, a lake, or a stream that flows, ever singing, on.

The trees which brave the heights and maintain the forest frontier among the storms, are the Engelmann spruce, sub-alpine fir, arctic willow, black birch, quaking aspen, and limber pine. For the most part, timber-line is a trifle above eleven thousand feet, but in a few places the trees climb up almost to twelve thousand. Most of the trees at timber-line are distorted and stunted by the hard conditions. Snow covers and crushes them; cold chains their activity through the greater part of the year; the high winds drain their sap, persecute them with relentless sand-blasts, and break their limbs and roots.

Among glacier-records in the Rocky Mountains those on the slopes of Long's Peak are pre-eminent for magnitude and interest. On the western slope of this peak the ice stream descended into the upper end of Glacier Gorge, where it united with streams from Mt. Barrat and McHenry Peak. Here it flowed northward for two miles through the now wonderfully ice-carved Glacier Gorge. Beyond the gorge heavy ice rivers flooded down to this ice stream from Thatch-Top, Taylor, Otis, and Hallett Peaks. A mile beyond the gorge it was deflected to the east by the solid slopes of Flat-Top and Mt. Hallett. It descended to about the altitude of eight thousand feet. Along its lower course, the lateral moraine on the south side dammed up a number of small water channels that drained the northern slope of Battle Mountain.

On the northern slope of the Peak a boulder field begins at the altitude of thirteen thousand feet and descends over a wide field, then over a terraced slope. Though probably not of great depth, it will average a mile wide and extends four miles down the slope. It contains an immense amount of material, enough to form a great mountain-peak. Probably the greatest array of glacial débris is the Mills Moraine on the east side of the Peak. This covers several thousand acres, consists of boulders, rock-fragments, and rock-flour, and in places is several hundred feet deep.

Where has all this wreckage come from? Some geologists have expressed the opinion that ages ago Long's Peak was two thousand or so feet higher. At the time of its great height, Long's Peak was united with the near surrounding peaks, — Meeker, Washington, and Storm, — and all stood together as one peak. The present shattered condition of these peaks, their crumbling nature, the mountain masses of débris on the slopes below, all of which must have come from heights above, suggest this explanation. But to take it as it now is, to stand on this crumbling peak to-day and look down upon the lakes, moraines, polished gorges, — all the vast and varied glacial works and ruins, — is for the geological student startling and profoundly eloquent.

Above the altitude of thirteen thousand feet are many fields of "eternal snow," and a dozen miles to the south of Long's Peak is the Arapahoe Glacier; while northward are the Andrews, Sprague, and Hallett Glaciers within ten miles. Though all these are small, each exhibits in a striking manner the Ice Age in a nutshell. On the east side of Long's Peak, too, is a moving ice-field that might well be classed as a glacier. By this ice begins the upper extent of the Mills Moraine, and in the gorge just below — one of the most utterly wild places on the earth — is Chasm Lake.

Most of the glacier lakes are in gorges or on terraces between the altitudes of eleven thousand and twelve thousand feet. Almost all have a slope or steep rising above them, down which the ice descended while gouging out their basins.

Grand Lake, one of the largest reservoirs constructed by the Ice King in the Rocky Mountains, is three miles in length and one in width, cut into bed-rock. This lake is less than nine thousand feet above the sea. It is in the eastern extremity of Middle Park, a few miles to the west of Long's Peak. Great peaks rising from it, a great moraine sweeping along its northerly and westerly shores, it peacefully shows the titanic beautifying landscape labors of the ice.

The glacial winter is over. The present snowfall over this section is about one half that of the Alps. Here snow-line is thirteen thousand feet above the sea, while in the Alps it is four thousand feet lower. Down from the heights of all the high peaks pour many white streams ever singing the song of the sea.

In these mountains there are many deep gorges and cañons. Most of these are short and ice-polished. The Thompson Cañon is one of the longest and finest. Its twenty miles of walled length is full of scenic contrasts and picturesque varieties. The lovely mingles with the wild. In places its walls stand two thousand feet above the river and the daisies. The walls are many-formed, rugged, polished, perpendicular, terraced, and statuesque, and are adorned with panels of rusty veneer, with decorative lichen tracery or with vertical meadows of velvet moss. Blossoms fill many niches with poetry, while shrubbery, concealing in its clinging the cracks in the wall, forms many a charming festoon.

In some stretches the parallel walls go straight away, well separated; then they curve, or crowd so closely that there is barely room for the river and the road. At intervals the walls sweep outward in short, grand semicircles and inclose ideal wild gardens of pines, grass, flowers, and the winding river. The river is ever varying its speed, its surface, and its song. Here it is a boulder-framed mirror reflecting the aspens and the sky, there a stretch of foam-flow; now it rests in a wild pool pierced with sharp rocks, now it hurries on to plunge and roar over a terrace of rocks, then on, always on, toward the sea.

The Spell of the Rockies

Speckled and rainbow trout dart in the streams. Mountain sheep climb and pose on the crags; bear, deer, and mountain lions are still occasionally seen prowling the woods or hurrying across the meadows. The wise coyote is also occasionally seen darting under cover, and he is frequently heard during the night. Here among the evergreens is found that wee and audacious bit of intensely interesting and animated life, the Frémont squirrel, and also, one of the dearest of all small animals, the merry chipmunk. Within this territory are a number of beaver colonies, whose ways I have described in earlier chapters.

The entire region is a wild-flower garden. Bloom-time lasts all summer long. The scores of streams which splash down from the snows are fringed with ferns and blossoms. There are many areas petalled with red, blue, purple, and gold. Difference of altitude, topography, and moisture-distribution induce nearly a thousand varieties to bloom in and to color this glad wild garden. July is white with Mariposa lilies. Wild roses, sweet peas, daisies, tiger lilies, violets, orchids, primroses, fringed blue gentians give

346

their color and their perfume to the friendly air. Here flourishes the Rocky Mountain columbine.

The region is gladdened with many kinds of birds. On the heights lives the serene, self-contained ptarmigan; the "camp-bird" resides in the upland forests; hummingbirds flit here and there; the robin sings and re-sings its song over the lowlands; blackbirds swing on the willows by the brooks; the wise magpie spreads his spotted wings and explores every corner. Along the cascading streams is the darling bird of the Rockies, the cheerful water-ouzel. Here, too, the hermit thrush charms the air with a wonderful wealth of melody, and here the solitaire, perhaps the most inspiring of all songsters, pours his divine melody amid pines, crags, and the sounds of winds and falling waters.

Numerous trails wind through this region, and over these one may visit Specimen Mountain, an old volcano, Fern and Odessa Lakes, — splendid tree-bordered alpine tarns, — Wild Basin, Locke Vale, Wind River, Glacier Gorge, and the summit of Long's Peak. The Flat-Top trail is the greatest one; this touches a variety of scenes, crosses the continental divide at twelve thousand feet, and connects Grand Lake and Estes Park.

This splendid natural recreation - ground might well "be held for the use of the people." It is close to the geographical centre of the country, is easily accessible, has an excellent climate, and as a National Park it would become a scenic resource of enormous and exhaustless richness.

THE END

Notes

Notes are keyed to page and line numbers. For example, 4:3 means page 4, line 3.

Frontispiece. This photograph of Longs Peak, like the others in this volume, was taken by Enos Mills.

"Racing an Avalanche"

5:16–17. John Tyndall (1820–1893), the noted British scientist and mountaineer, who was one of the first to investigate the motion of glaciers, published his *Hours of Exercise in the Alps* in 1871. Tyndall Glacier, one of the five true glaciers in Rocky Mountain National Park, lying between Hallett Peak and Flattop Mountain, honors Tyndall's contribution to the study of glaciers and glaciation. Though the name was not officially adopted by the National Park Service until 1932, the original suggestion apparently came from Enos Mills.

5:18. Robert Burns (1759–1796), the Scottish poet.

6. The photograph facing this page was taken just outside of Telluride, a mining camp located in the San Juan Mountains of southwestern Colorado.

13:21. The town of Aspen, located in the valley (gulch) of the Roaring River just west of the Continental Divide in west-central Colorado, became a prosperous mining center following the discovery of silver in 1879. By 1893 Aspen had become the third largest city in Colorado. Its population in 1900 was just over 3,300.

"Little Conservationists"

20. The photograph facing this page is of Mt. Meeker (13,911 feet), the second highest peak in what is now Rocky Mountain National Park. See 207:2.

20:23. The Moraine Colony was one of several beaver colonies located on the lower flanks of Longs Peak not far from Enos Mills's Longs Peak Inn and homestead cabin. One of Mills's favorite pastimes over the years was accompanying his guests to these beaver ponds, where he entertained them with impromptu lectures. Mills knew his subject well. His book *In Beaver World* (1913) was the first important work on the animal since Lewis H. Morgan's classic study of 1865.

28:12. Though the beaver are returning to Rocky Mountain National Park, the mountain lion is extinct. At the turn of the century, however, mountain lions inhabited the Tahosa Valley and early residents remembered hearing them roar in the night. An area to the north of Longs Peak Inn (southeast of Estes Cone) was once known as Lion Gulch.

32:23. The Arapaho Indians, who regarded the mountain valleys along Colorado's Front Range as their hunting grounds, told stories of trapping buffalo in the Estes Park region. Early settlers reported the occasional discovery of bison skulls and Indian artefacts.

33:3–4. The lines quoted are from the second, 1868, edition (XLVII, 1–2) of the Edward Fitzgerald (1809–1883) translation of *The Rubaiyat of Omar Khayyam*.

35:11. Though prospectors did wander in from time to time to try their luck, the absence of gold and silver saved the scenery of Estes Park from being defaced by the kind of mining activity that left the slopes and gulleys in and around Central City and Blackhawk to the south permanently scarred with shaft openings and piles of tailings.

"Harvest Time with Beavers"

51:6. Mills Moraine, named after Enos Mills.

"Mountain-Top Weather"

75:18–19. Granite Pass, on the saddle between Battle Mountain (12,044 feet) and Mount Lady Washington (13,281 feet), marks the intersection of two trails to the Boulder Field on Longs Peak: one originates in Glacier Gorge, the other in the Tahosa Valley, near Longs Peak Inn.

81:15. Enos Mills erected his homestead cabin in 1885–1886 in the Tahosa Valley, then Longs Peak Valley, at the very foot of the peak.

87:2–3. John Muir (1838–1914), the Scottish-born explorer, naturalist, and writer who served as Mills's lifelong inspiration. As noted in the Introduction, the two men first met in December 1889 during a chance encounter on the beach near San Francisco. The source of the quotation that follows, however, is unclear.

87:14–15. Mills's first volume of nature essays, published at Boston by Houghton Mifflin in 1909. A new edition, with an introduction and notes by the present editor, was published by the University of Nebraska Press in 1988.

88:7. Mt. Teller (12,602 feet) is located in Summit County in central Colorado. It was named after Henry M. Teller (1830–1914) of Colorado, who served five terms in the United States Senate.

"Rob of the Rockies"

95:18. The Cache la Poudre River flows northeast out of Poudre Lake, which is located to the east of the Continental Divide at Milner Pass. According to tradition, the Poudre River was named in 1836 by a party of French trappers from St. Louis who over the course of one winter safely deposited some of their supplies, including a quantity of black gunpowder, close by its banks.

98:15. The gold and silver mining town of Leadville is located in central Colorado near the headwaters of the Arkansas River just east of the Continental Divide. Following the discovery of silver in 1875, Leadville became one of the most glamorous, profitable, and wide-open mining camps in Colorado. In 1900 it boasted a population of 12,455.

101:10. Lieutenant Zebulon M. Pike (1779–1813) was the first official American explorer to enter Colorado. Pike and his party of twenty-three men, which had been dispatched from St. Louis with instructions to explore the headwaters of the Arkansas and Red rivers and to reconnoitre the Spanish settlements in New Mexico, sighted Pikes Peak on November 15, 1906, and made an unsuccessful attempt to climb it. From there Pike and his men explored South Park and the sources of the Arkansas River and then turned south to cross, as Mills notes, the Wet Mountains and the Sangre de Cristo Mountains, via Medano Pass, before being taken into custody by Spanish troops in New Mexico and escorted to Santa Fe.

102:5. Horn Peak (13,450 feet) is located in the northern section of the Sangre de Cristo Mountains.

103:5. Medano Pass (10,200 feet), located northwest of Gardner. As noted above, Zebulon Pike used Medano Pass in crossing the Sangre de Cristo Mountains.

103:18. Sierra Blanca (14,363 feet), the highest peak in Sangre de Cristo Mountains of south-central Colorado and the fourth highest in the state. At one time Sierra Blanca was thought to be the highest peak in the United States and consequently became the objective of a number of early mountaineers. The first recorded ascent was by two members of the Wheeler Survey party in 1874.

"Sierra Blanca"

112:8–9. Mt. Elbert (14,433 feet), located in the Sawatch Range of cen-

tral Colorado some twelve miles southwest of Leadville, is the highest
mountain in the state.

112:12–13. Fort Garland, located on Trinchera Creek in the San Luis
Valley just west of the Sangre de Cristo Mountains, was established as a
military post in 1858. In 1866–1867 it was commanded by Kit Carson
(1809–1868), the famous trapper and guide turned Indian agent and
soldier.

112:19. An allusion to Mills's assignment during the winters of 1903 to
1906 as Colorado's official State Snow Observer. In this capacity it was
Mills's assignment to "traverse the upper slopes of the Rockies"—one
winter he actually walked the length of the Continental Divide from the
Wyoming line south to New Mexico—measuring the snow accumulation
at the headwaters of streams in order to anticipate the ensuing spring
and summer runoff.

117:4. The broad and flat San Luis Valley of south-central Colorado
runs from northwest to southeast for a distance of some 125 miles. On
the east it is bounded by the Sangre de Cristo Mountains, to the west by
the San Juans.

"The Wealth of the Woods"

127:22. Louis George Carpenter (1861–1935), a native of Michigan,
joined the faculty of Colorado Agricultural College (now Colorado State
University) in 1888 to teach irrigation engineering and to conduct irrigation experiments at the Colorado Agricultural Experiment Station. At
CAC Carpenter earned a national reputation by organizing the first systematic instructional and research program in irrigation engineering, a
subject of critical importance to the water-starved West. Between 1903
and 1905, he served as state engineer of Colorado and in this capacity he
engaged the services of Enos Mills as State Snow Observer. See 112:19.

128:21–22. The source of the quotation is John Muir's *The Mountains
of California* (New York: The Century Co., 1894), p. 192.

"The Forest Fire"

140:22. Now called the Never Summer Range.

140:24. The Grand River is the former name given to the upper portion of the Colorado River, which has its source in what is now the north-
western corner of Rocky Mountain National Park and flows south
through Middle Park. The name was officially changed in 1921.

"Dr. Woodpecker, Tree-Surgeon"

200:2–3. Frank M. Chapman (1864–1945) was a noted ornithologist and the author of the first dependable modern guide to birds, *Handbook of the Birds of the Eastern United States* (1895). In 1899 Chapman became founding editor of *Bird-Lore*, the official organ of the National Audubon Society, which quickly became the foremost popular bird magazine in the country. Chapman, who spent some fifty-five years as associate curator and then curator of ornithology at New York's American Museum of Natural History, made one brief visit to Estes Park, where he and Mills met.

"Little Boy Grizzly"

207:2. Mt. Meeker (13,911 feet), which lies directly to the south of Longs Peak, is named for Nathan Meeker (1817–1879), the agricultural editor of Horace Greeley's *New York Tribune* and a social reformer, who in 1869 came west to organize and run Union Colony, the agricultural cooperative which became the town of Greeley. Meeker himself was killed by Utes during the White River Massacre in September 1879.

209:1. Both Enos Mills and his younger brother Enoch "Joe" Mills (1880–1935) claimed exclusive credit for the 1903 capture and rearing of the two bear cubs Jenny and Johnny and their subsequent relocation to the Denver Zoo. Enos Mills told the story here and again in his book, *The Grizzly: Our Greatest Wild Animal* (Boston: Houghton Mifflin, 1919, pp. 101–15). Joe Mills told the story of Jenny and Johnny both in "My Friend the Grizzlies," *St. Nicholas*, 41 (February 1914): 294–97 and in *A Mountain Boyhood* (New York: J. H. Sears & Company, Inc., 1926), pp. 275–80). The fact that neither brother mentions the other is atttributable to a quarrel that irrevocably estranged them in 1908. The truth of the matter, undoubtedly, is that the original capture of the bear cubs was a joint enterprise that became parochial only in retrospect. As a writer for the *Denver Post* noted in his July 22, 1936, story of Jenny's death:

> Jennie [sic] was born in the wilds of what is now Rocky Mountain National park in January 1903. The late Joseph and Enos Mills, longtime residents of the region and Colorado naturalists, had a string of traps out for coyotes. Jennie, a cub, was caught.
>
> What became of the mother is a mystery, but Jack, her brother, refused to desert her and was captured with her. He died ten years ago [1925]. Both bears were sold to the zoo, and, according to the late Joe Mills's story of the catch, as told to Hill [Clyde E. Hill, whose

father Alfred E. Hill (1850–1918) worked for the Denver Zoo from 1890 to 1912, the greatest part of the time as super-intendent], the $225 they brought went toward Mills' education at the University of Colorado. (p.16)

How or why Jack became Johnny, however, remains unclear.

213:3. Scotch was Enos Mills's collie, which he received as a puppy in 1902. The dog soon became his constant companion and a fixture at Longs Peak Inn. Scotch had been taught to put out fires, and his death in 1910 occurred because the dog tried to extinguish the fuse on a charge of dynamite being used by a local road crew. Mills celebrated the deeds of his dog in a chapter ("Faithful Scotch") in *Wild Life on the Rockies* (1909). This chapter was subsequently expanded into a magazine article, "The Story of Scotch," which he published in the May 1, 1912 issue of *Country Life in America*, and then into book form, *The Story of Scotch* (Boston: Houghton Mifflin, 1916).

"Alone with a Landslide"

223:3. The Uncompahgre Mountains are a subrange of the San Juans of southwestern Colorado, lying east of the Uncompahgre River and north of the upper Lake Fork of the Gunnison River.

223:7–8. Lake City, in the heart of the San Juans, is located on the up-per Lake Fork of the Gunnison River, fifty-five miles southwest of Gun-nison. It became a boom town with the discovery of gold and silver in the mid-1870s. Gold production peaked in 1895, and by 1900 the boom was over and Lake City's population had declined to some 700.

224:13. Uncompahgre Peak (14,306 feet), which dominates the north-east corner of the San Juans, is located some eight miles from Lake City. It is the ninth highest mountain in Colorado.

226:11. As Mills notes below, Ridgway, located on Uncompahgre River eleven miles northwest of Ouray, was a prosperous railroad town serving the mines of southwestern Colorado. In 1900 it had a population of 245.

228:8–9. The Little Cimarron is the name given to the left-branch of the Gunnison River, located in Gunnison County.

228:16. Mt. Coxcomb (13,663 feet) is located near the sources of the Middle and West forks of the Cimarron River.

237:3. The Gunnison joins the Colorado at Grand Junction.

242:19. Courthouse Mountain (12,152 feet) is located to the north of Mount Coxcomb.

243:4. Mills is undoubtedly referring to Chimney Peak (11,781 feet), which stands just north of Courthouse Mountain.

"The Maker of Scenery and Soil"

248:15. Muir devotes several chapters of *The Mountains of California* (1894) to the effects of glaciation. See 250:10.

249:1. The seven hills of ancient Rome.

250:11–18. *The Mountains of California*, p. 197.

250:19–24. The quotation is from Junius Henderson's essay "Extinct and Existing Glaciers of Colorado" (p. 36), published in volume 9 of *University of Colorado Studies* (Boulder, 1910), pp. 33–76. Its author, "Judge" Junius Henderson (1865–1937) was a lawyer-turned-scientist who earned a considerable reputation as one of Colorado's early naturalists. After being admitted to the state bar in 1894, Henderson practiced law in Boulder until 1902. A year later he became the first curator (unpaid) of the natural history museum at the University of Colorado and took up a new career as a professor of natural history which would span the next thirty years. One of Henderson's interests was glaciation. He helped discover and then explored Fair and Isabelle Glaciers in the Indian Peaks west of Boulder. The work cited by Mills was for many years the standard work on the subject. Interestingly enough, Henderson's essay cites Mills's *The Story of Estes Park and a Guide Book* (Denver, 1905) as "especially useful because of the accompanying map which gives the location of the principal mountain peaks and named ice-fields in the region north and northwest of Long's Peak" (p. 51).

250: The photograph facing this page is of the Hallett Glacier (or Rowe Glacier as it is now known), a large crescent of ice partly surrounding a small tarn, which sits below Hagues Peak in the north-central part of Rocky Mountain National Park. Professor George H. Stone (1841–1917) visited the glacier during the summer of 1887, and reported its discovery in an article, "A Living Glacier on Hague's Peak," which he published in the September 23, 1887, issue of *Science*. Though Stone named the glacier after William Hallett (1851–1941), one of Estes Park's pioneering mountaineers, who had visited the glacier about 1883 and told Stone of its location, the name was changed by the U.S. Board of Geographic Names in June 1932 to honor Israel Rowe (?-1884), a guide and hunter, who made the original discovery in the late 1870s. Mills recorded his own first visit of 1895 in "A Canyon in Ice," published in *Outdoor Life* in 1898.

251:5. Arapaho Glacier, located in the Indian Peaks Wilderness Area of the Roosevelt National Forest, south of Rocky Mountain National Park and some twenty miles west of Boulder, is the largest active glacier in Colorado. Junius Henderson, who Mills cites above (see note 250: 19–24), published a series of articles on the Arapaho Glacier during the first decade of the twentieth century.

253:17. Grand Lake, the largest natural lake in Colorado, forms part of the western boundary of Rocky Mountain National Park.

255:22. In 1820, Dr. Joseph Hamel (1788–1862), a Russian-born scientific writer and physician, two Oxford students, and eight guides were overwhelmed by an avalanche as they ascended Mont Blanc, and three of the guides were lost when they fell into a crevasse. The source of Mills's information on the episode (and the "interesting story" alluded to below) are unclear, though the Hamel tragedy and its sequel inspired a number of literary efforts, including John Ruskin's poem "The Avalanche" (1835).

260:8. Glacial fissures.

260:20. There are in fact two Arapaho Peaks flanking the Arapaho Glacier: North Arapaho Peak (13,502 feet) and South Arapaho Peak (13,397 feet).

263:1. Edward Orton, Jr. (1865–1932), as a member of the Ohio State University Department of Chemistry carried out his geological survey of Mills Morraine and the Longs Peak region during the summer of 1908. Orton subsequently delivered a paper on the subject at the December 1908 meetings of the American Association for the Advancement of Science at the Johns Hopkins University. A brief abstract of this paper was published as "The Mills Moraine, with Some General Remarks on the Glaciation of the Long's Peak Region of Colorado," *Science*, N.S., 29 (1909), 751–52. Mt. Orton (11,724 feet) in Wild Basin is named after Professor Orton's father, Edward Orton, Sr. (1829–1899), the president of both Antioch College and the Ohio State University and from 1882 to 1899 Ohio's state geologist. The quotation below may well be from Orton's 1908 paper, though it does not appear in the published abstract.

"A Rainy Day at the Stream's Source"

267:7–8. The north branch of the St. Vrain River originates in Wild Basin to the south of Longs Peak, flows east and northeast past Lyons and Longmont, and empties into the South Platte.

267:13. Undoubtedly the fire which broke out during the summer of 1902 along the North St. Vrain River. For a week the fire raged out of control, without any attempt to contain it, thus endangering the water supply of some 38,000 acres of farmland around Longmont. Enos Mills provided photographs for an article describing the fire that was published in the February 4, 1903, edition of the *Denver Times*.

268:24. The fork of the two branches of the Saint Vrain River. See 271:19–21.

269:19. The water-ouzel (or water thrush), a plump bluish gray bird with a wrenlike tail that frequents swift mountain streams and cascades, was one of Enos Mills's favorite birds. During his early explorations of Wild Basin, he came across the water ouzel in several locations and named Ouzel Lake in the bird's honor.

"A Midget in Fur"

323:8–10. Muir devotes an entire chapter of *The Mountains of California* (1894) to the Douglas squirrel.

"The Estes Park Region"

337:5. Helen Hunt (1830–1885), or Helen Hunt Jackson as she became following her second marriage in 1875, a native of Amherst, Massachusetts, earned a minor reputation as a writer of popular poetry and fiction, and about the novel *Ramona* (1884). Her enthusiastic essays about the scenic wonders of the American West and about her new life in the Colorado Territory, where she had moved for reasons of health in 1873, were collected and published in 1878 as *Bits of Travel at Home*. Helen Hunt Jackson later became the champion of the displaced American Indian in *A Century of Dishonor* (1881) and in the letters and essays which she wrote for newspapers and magazines.

337:5. Anna Dickinson (1842–1932), a well-known author and lecturer, on September 13, 1873, became the first woman to climb to the top of Longs Peak when she made the ascent with members of the Hayden Survey.

337:6. Isabella Bird (1831–1904), a plucky Englishwoman, recorded her adventures in Estes Park climaxing in the October 1873 ascent of Longs Peak in the company of the legendary desperado "Rocky Mountain Jim" Nugent (c. 1828–1874) in her book *A Lady's Life in the Rocky Mountains* (London: John Murray, 1879).

337:17. Grace Greenwood was the pseudonym for Sara Jane Lippincott (1823–1904), a writer of poetry, travel essays, juvenalia, and popular biography. Lippincott frequently vacationed in Colorado and became an enthusiastic promoter of the Rocky Mountain region, most particularly in the essays which she collected and published in *New Life in New Lands: Notes of Travel* (1873). The comparison that Mills cites is from this volume (p. 41).

338. The photograph facing this page, one of Mills's most famous, was taken from Mt. Olympus (8,808 feet), which stands at the eastern entrance to Estes Park.

339:23. Park, in the parlance of the mountains, means valley. Allen's park lies at the southeastern entrance to Rocky Mountain National Park. The present village of Allenspark—named after Alonzo Allen, an early settler who built a cabin nearby in 1864—is spelled as one word.

341:14. Mt. Barrat is the early name given to Chiefs Head Peak (13,579 feet), to the west of Longs Peak.

341:15. McHenrys Peak (13,327 feet), located in the Glacier Gorge region of Rocky Mountain National Park, is named after Benjamin F. McHenry (1837–1915), an 1869 graduate of Oberlin College who for many years served as a professor of mathematics and natural science at Union Christian College in Merom, Indiana. During the early 1880s McHenry and his family spent three summers in the Estes Park region. Though McHenry and his son Howard hiked to Grand Lake by way of Specimen Mountain and then returned to Estes Park over the Flattop trail, they failed to climb the unnamed peak that would one day bear his name. "We failed to accomplish what we set out to do," he wrote in 1898, "but we did not fail. We were all the while in country grand beyond description."

341:19. Taylor Peak (13,153 feet), like Otis and Hallett peaks, lies along the Continental Divide to the northwest of McHenrys Peak. It is named after Albert Reynolds Taylor (1846–1929), president of Kansas State Normal School in Emporia, Kansas, from 1882 to 1901, who visited Estes Park with his family during the summer of 1895.

341:19. Otis Peak (12,586 feet) is named after Dr. Edward Osgood Otis (1848–1933), a Boston physician with an interest in climatology who for many years served on the faculty of Tufts College. Otis climbed with Frederick Chapin and his party during the summer of 1887 and in the process named Hallett Peak in honor of their guide. See Note 250. Chapin records their experiences in his delightful *Mountaineering in Colorado: The Peaks about Estes Park* (Boston: Appalachian Mountain Club, 1889), since reissued (1987) by the University of Nebraska Press with a foreword and notes by the present editor.

341:19. Hallett Peak (12,713 feet). See note above.

342:2. Battle Mountain (12,044 feet), one of the near neighbors of Longs Peak to the northwest, was so-named by Enos Mills because it so obviously bore the scars of the forces of nature, including an early forest fire.

343:12–13. Arapaho Glacier: See 251:5.

343:12–14. There are five "true" or living glaciers within the area embraced by Rocky Mountain National Park. In addition to the three noted here (Andrews, Sprague, and Hallett [Rowe] glaciers), there are Tyndall Glacier, lying in the gorge between Flattop Mountain and Hallett Peak

(See 5:16–17), and Mills Glacier, below the East Face of Longs Peak, named for Enos Mills. Andrews Glacier, which is located between Taylor Peak and Otis Peak, was named by Estes Park pioneer Abner E. Sprague (1850–1943) after his relative by marriage, Edwin B. Andrews. Sprague Glacier, which lies below Stones Peak in the west-central part of Rocky Mountain National Park, was named after Abner Sprague by Enos Mills in 1905.

344:22. The Thompson Canyon is named after the river that flows through it. In 1903 a road was completed through the Canyon linking Loveland and Estes Park. It replaced the older Bald Mountain Road which made its way through Rattlesnake Park, over Pole Hill, and emerged in Estes Park where the Crocker Ranch now stands.

346:3. Mills deliberately omits elk which, though native to the region and once plentiful, had all but been wiped out by uncontrolled hunting during the 1870s and 1880s. Elk were reintroduced in 1913 when the residents of Estes Park raised funds to purchase a herd of twenty-nine from Montana. An additional herd of twenty-four elk were added in 1915, the year that Rocky Mountain National Park was dedicated. Thanks to their protected status, the elk are once again abundant.

347:19–20. Specimen Mountain (12,489 feet) and the adjacent Crater to the southwest (both of which lie immediately north of Milner Pass) were once believed to be part of an extinct volcano. Geologists have now established that both features were formed of ash and other volcanic material from an eruption that took place elsewhere.

Index

361

Index

Index

Index

Index

Index